wucius wong **Principles of Two-Dimensional Design**

JOHN WILEY & SONS, INC.

New York   Chichester   Weinheim   Brisbane   Singapore   Toronto

Designed by Wucius Wong

Library of Congress Catalog Card Number 72-1854

ISBN 0-471-28960-4

Printed in the United States of America

98 99 OZ 30 29 28 27 26 25 24

CONTENTS

Chapter 1   Introduction   5
Chapter 2   Form   9
Chapter 3   Repetition   15
Chapter 4   Structure   23
Chapter 5   Similarity   33
Chapter 6   Gradation   39
Chapter 7   Radiation   49
Chapter 8   Anomaly   61
Chapter 9   Contrast   67
Chapter 10   Concentration   75
Chapter 11   Texture   79
Chapter 12   Space   89

PREFACE

The present book is the result of my past several years of teaching two-dimensional design at the Chinese University of Hong Kong, Department of Extramural Studies. It was not a course for students of the university proper, but for members of the public who wished to learn design fundamentals in their spare time. The quality of my students, who had varied backgrounds, was thus rather uneven. Nearly all of them worked in the daytime, and they could easily drop the course if they did not like it. The class met once a week in the evenings, two hours a session for twelve sessions. When the course first opened in 1966, Hong Kong had practically no organized design training at all.

The course was conducted in ordinary classrooms without studio facilities. It was planned in such a way that there was one exercise required after each lecture, to be handed in at the beginning of the next session and discussed. All exercises were done at home, and each exercise demanded about five to eight hours.

Over the years the course was repeated four or five times. When I first taught the subject, my design theories were far from formulated. The content of the course was revised every time I retaught it. Even as I wrote this book, many alterations and modifications were still being made on my previous lectures.

What I am after is to develop some kind of visual logic by which students can be led to understand the elements of design, the possibilities of organizing them, and the limitations. Instead of describing the usual vague terms we encounter in aesthetics, I hope to present definite and concrete situations, each with infinite variations for one to explore.

So the book deals with concepts of forms and structures, covering most situations in two-dimensional composition, formal or informal. The more formal kinds of composition occupy the greater part of the book because they are, in my belief, the basic disciplines which a beginner in design must understand thoroughly. There is no shortcut to designing, but with this book perhaps students may be guided towards an analytic attitude and a clearer vision.

The color aspects of design and three-dimensional design are beyond the scope of this book; they will form the subjects of future studies.

I wish to thank many of my students whose works are included in the book; Mr. Cheung Shu-sun who designed the cover; Mr. Leung Kui-ting who helped with the photography; Mr. John Warner, Curator of the City Museum and Art Gallery, Hong Kong, who encouraged me to do the teaching outside my regular museum duties; Mr. T. C. Lai, Director of Extramural Studies of the Chinese University of Hong Kong, who always takes a keen interest in my courses; and lastly but not the least, Mr. Porter A. McCray, Director of Asian Cultural Program, J.D.R. 3rd Fund, New York, who provided me with the opportunity of a fellowship which enabled me to revisit the United States in 1970-71, resulting in many fresh inspirations.

The book is specially dedicated to my wife Pansy, who has helped, among other things, in the typing of the manuscript, the preparation of all the diagrams, and the general layout of the book.

W.W.

CHAPTER 1: INTRODUCTION

What Is Design?

Many people would think of design as some kind of effort in beautifying the outward appearance of things. Certainly mere beautification is one aspect of design, but design is much more than this.

Look around us. Design is not just ornamentation. The well-designed chair not only has a pleasing outward appearance, but stands firmly on the ground and provides adequate comfort for whoever sits on it. Furthermore, it should be safe and quite durable, able to be produced at a comparatively economic cost, packed and shipped conveniently, and, of course, it should have a specific function, whether for working, resting, dining, or other human activities.

Design is a process of purposeful visual creation. Unlike painting and sculpture, which are the realization of artists' personal visions and dreams, design fills practical needs. A piece of graphic design has to be placed before the eyes of the public and to convey a predetermined message. An industrial product has to meet consumers' requirements.

A good design, in short, is the best possible visual expression of the essence of "something," whether this be a message or a product. To do this faithfully and effectively, the designer should look for the best possible way this "something" can be shaped, made, distributed, used, and related to the environment. His creation should not only be just aesthetic but also functional, while reflecting or guiding the taste of the time.

The Visual Language

Design is practical. The designer is a practical man. But before he is ready to tackle practical problems, he has to master a visual language.

This visual language is the basis of design creation. Setting aside the functional aspect of design, there are principles, rules, or concepts in respect of visual organization that may concern a designer. A designer can work without conscious knowledge of any of these principles, rules, or concepts, because his personal taste and sensitivity to visual relationships are much more important, but a thorough understanding of them would definitely enhance his capability in visual organization.

In the first year's curriculum of every art school or university art department, regardless of the fields of specialization the students are to follow later, there is always a course variously called Basic Design, Fundamental Design, Two-Dimensional Design, etc., which deals with the grammar of this visual language.

Interpreting the Visual Language

There are numerous ways of interpreting the visual language. Unlike the spoken or written language of which the grammatical laws are more or less established, the visual language has no obvious laws. Each design theorist may have a completely different set of discoveries.

My own interpretations, as unfolded in this book, may appear to be much on the rigid side and oversimplified. Readers will soon find that my theorization has a lot to do with systematic thinking and very little to do with emotion and intuition. This is because I prefer to tackle the principles in precise and concrete terms with maximum objectivity and minimum ambiguity.

We must not forget that the designer is a problem-solving person. The problems he is to face are always given. This means that he cannot alter any of the problems but must find appropriate solutions. Certainly an inspired solution can be attained intuitively, but in most cases the designer has to rely on his enquiring mind, which probes into all the possible visual situations within the requirements of individual problems.

Elements of Design

My theorization begins with a list of elements

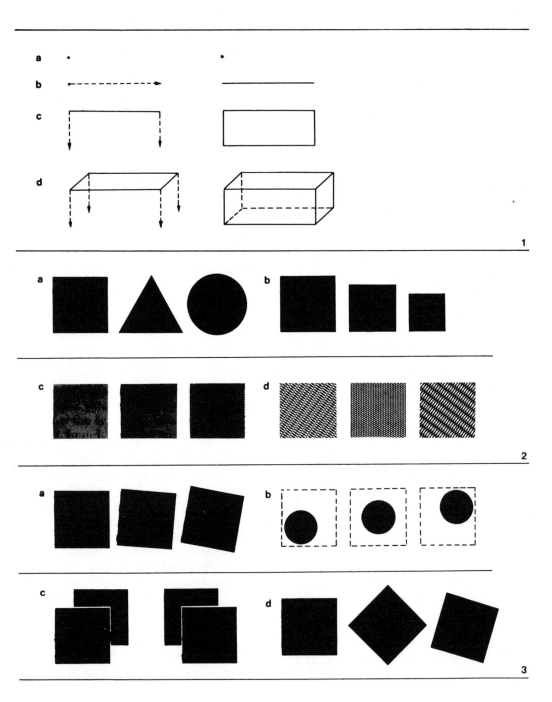

of design. This list is necessary because the elements will form the basis of all our future discussions.

The elements are, in fact, very much related to each other and cannot be easily separated in our general visual experience. Tackled individually, they may appear rather abstract, but together they determine the ultimate appearance and contents of a design.

Four groups of elements are distinguished:
(a) conceptual elements
(b) visual elements
(c) relational elements
(d) practical elements

Conceptual Elements

Conceptual elements are not visible. They do not actually exist but seem to be present. For instance, we feel that there is a point at the angle of a shape, there is a line marking the contour of an object, there are planes enveloping volume, and volume occupying space. These points, lines, planes, and volumes are not really there; if they are really there, they are no longer conceptual.

(a) **Point** — A point indicates position. It has no length or breadth. It does not occupy any area of space. It is the beginning and end of a line, and is where two lines meet or intersect. (Fig. **1a**)

(b) **Line** — As a point moves, its path becomes a line. A line has length but no breadth. It has position and direction. It is bound by points. It forms the border of a plane. (Fig. **1b**)

(c) **Plane** — The path of a line in motion (in a direction other than its intrinsic direction) becomes a plane. A plane has length and breadth, but no thickness. It has position and direction. It is bound by lines. It defines the external limits of a volume. (Fig. **1c**)

(d) **Volume** — The path of a plane in motion (in a direction other than its intrinsic direction) becomes a volume. It has position in space and is bound by planes. In two-dimensional design, volume is illusory. (Fig. **1d**)

Visual Elements

When we draw an object on paper, we employ a line that is visible to represent a line that is conceptual. The visible line not only has length but also breadth. Its color and texture are determined by the materials we use and the way we use them.

Thus, when conceptual elements become visible, they have shape, size, color, and texture. Visual elements form the most prominent part of a design because they are what we can actually see.

(a) **Shape** — Anything that can be seen has a shape which provides the main identification in our perception. (Fig. **2a**)

(b) **Size** — All shapes have size. Size is relative if we describe it in terms of bigness and smallness, but it is also physically measurable. (Fig. **2b**)

(c) **Color** — A shape is distinguished from its surroundings because of color. Color here is used in its broad sense, comprising not only all the hues of the spectrum but also the neutrals (black, white, and all the intermediate grays), and also all their tonal and chromatic variations. (Fig. **2c**)

(d) **Texture** — Texture refers to the surface characteristics of a shape. This may be plain or decorated, smooth or rough, and may appeal to the sense of touch as much as to sight. (Fig. **2d**)

Relational Elements

This group of elements governs the placement and interrelationship of the shapes in a design. Some are to be perceived, such as direction and position; some are to be felt, such as space and gravity.

(a) **Direction** — Direction of a shape depends on how it is related to the observer, to the frame that contains it, or to other shapes nearby. (Fig. **3a**)

(b) Position — The position of a shape is judged by its relationship to the frame or the structure (see Chapter 4) of the design. (Fig. **3b**)

(c) Space — Shapes of any size, however small, occupy space. Thus, space can be occupied or left blank. It can also be flat or illusory to suggest depth. (Fig. **3c**)

(d) Gravity — The sense of gravity is not visual but psychological. As we are pulled by the gravity of the earth, we tend to attribute heaviness or lightness, stability or instability to individual shapes or groups of shapes. (Fig. **3d**)

Practical Elements

The practical elements underlie the content and extension of a design. They are beyond the scope of this book, but I would like to mention them here:

(a) Representation — When a shape is derived from nature or the man-made world, it is representational. Representation may be realistic, stylized, or near-abstract.

(b) Meaning — Meaning is present when the design conveys a message.

(c) Function — Function is present when a design is to serve a purpose.

The Framal Reference

All the above elements normally exist within a boundary which we call a "framal reference." The framal reference marks the outer limits of a design and defines an area within which the created elements and left-over blank space, if any, all work together.

The framal reference is not necessarily an actual frame. If it is, then the frame should be considered as an integral part of the design. The visual elements of the visible frame should not be overlooked. If there is no actual frame, the edges of a poster, the page of a magazine, the various surfaces of a package all become framal references for the respective designs.

The framal reference of a design can be of any shape, though it is usually rectangular. The die-cut shape of a printed sheet is the framal reference of the design that is contained in it.

The Picture Plane

Within the framal reference lies the picture plane. The picture plane is actually the plane surface of the paper (or any other material) upon which the design is created.

Shapes are directly painted or printed on this picture plane, but they may appear to be above, below, or unparallel to it because of spatial illusions, which will be fully discussed in Chapter 12.

Form and Structure

All the visual elements constitute what we generally call "form," which is the primary concern in our present enquiry into the visual language. Form in this sense is not just a shape that is seen, but a shape of definite size, color, and texture.

The way form is created, constructed, or organized along with other forms is often governed by a certain discipline which we call "structure." Structure which involves the relational elements is also essential in our studies.

Both form and structure will be thoroughly discussed in the chapters to follow.

CHAPTER 2: FORM

Form and the Conceptual Elements

As already pointed out, the conceptual elements are not visible. Thus point, line, or plane, when visible, becomes form. A point on paper, however small, must have shape, size, color, and texture if it is meant to be seen. So must a line or a plane. Volume remains illusory in two-dimensional design.

Visible points, lines, or planes are forms in the true sense, although forms as points or lines are still simply called points or lines in common practice.

Form as Point

A form is recognized as a point because it is small.

Smallness, of course, is relative. A form may appear fairly large when it is confined in a tiny framal reference, but the same form may appear rather small when it is put inside a much greater framal reference. (Fig. 4)

The most common shape of a point is that of a circle which is simple, compact, non-angular, and non-directional. However, a point may be square, triangular, oval, or even of a somewhat irregular shape. (Fig. 5)

Thus the main characteristics of a point are: (a) its size should be comparatively small, and (b) its shape should be rather simple.

Form as Line

A form is recognized as a line because of two reasons: (a) its breadth is extremely narrow, and (b) its length is quite prominent.

A line generally conveys the feeling of thinness. Thinness, like smallness, is relative. The extreme ratio between length and breadth of a shape makes it a line, but there is no absolute criterion for this.

Three separate aspects should be considered in a line:

The overall shape — This refers to its general appearance, which is described as straight, curved, bent, irregular, or hand-drawn. (Fig. 6a)

The body — As a line has breadth, its body is contained within two edges. The shapes of these two edges and the relationship between them determine the shape of the body. Usually the two edges are smooth and parallel, but sometimes they may cause the body of the line to appear tapering, knotty, wavy, or irregular. (Fig. 6b)

The extremities — These may be negligible when the line is very thin. But if the line is quite broad, the shapes of its extremities may become prominent. They may be square, round, pointed, or any simple shape. (Fig. 6c)

Points arranged in a row may evoke the feeling of a line. But in this case the line is conceptual and not visual, for what we see is still a series of points. (Fig. 6d)

Form as Plane

On a two-dimensional surface, all flat forms that are not commonly recognized as points or lines are forms as plane.

A planar form is bound by conceptual lines which constitute the edges of the form. The characteristics of these conceptual lines and their interrelationships determine the shape of the planar form.

Planar forms have a variety of shapes, which may be classified as follows:

(a) **Geometric** — constructed mathematically. (Fig. 7a)

(b) **Organic** — bounded by free curves, suggesting fluidity and growth. (Fig. 7b)

(c) **Rectilinear** — bound by straight lines which are not related to one another mathematically. (Fig. 7c)

(d) **Irregular** — bound by straight and curved lines which are not related to one another mathematically. (Fig. 7d)

(e) **Hand-drawn** — calligraphic or created with the unaided hand. (Fig. 7e)

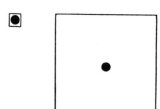

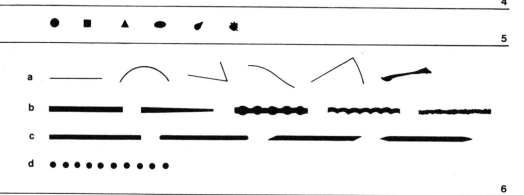

4

5

6

a

b

c

d

a

b

c

d

e

f

7

(f) **Accidental** — determined by the effect of special processes or materials, or obtained accidentally. (Fig. **7f**)

Planar forms may be suggested by means of outlining. In this case the thickness of the lines used should be considered. Points arranged in a row can also outline a planar form.

Points or lines densely and regularly grouped together can also suggest planar forms. They become the texture of the plane.

Form as Volume

Form as volume is completely illusory and demands a special spatial situation. A full discussion of this will be found in Chapter 12.

Positive and Negative Forms

Form is generally seen as occupying space, but it can also be seen as blank space surrounded by occupied space.

When it is perceived as occupying space, we call it "positive" form. When it is perceived as blank space surrounded by occupied space, we call it "negative" form. (Fig. **8**)

In black-and-white design, we tend to regard black as occupied and white as unoccupied. Thus, a black form is recognized as positive and a white form as negative. But such attributions are not always true. Especially when forms penetrate or intersect one another (see the section on the interrelationships of forms later in this chapter), what is positive and what is negative are no longer easily distinguishable.

Form, whether positive or negative, is commonly referred to as the "figure," which is on a "ground." Here "ground" denotes the area surrounding the form or the "figure." In ambiguous cases, the figure-ground relationship may be reversible. This will be discussed in Chapter 12.

Form and Color Distribution

Without changing any of the elements in a design, the distribution of colors within a definite color scheme can have a large range of variations. Let us have a very simple example. Suppose we have a form which exists within a frame, and we can only use black and white. Four different ways of color distribution can be obtained:

(a) white form on white ground (Fig. **9a**)
(b) white form on black ground (Fig. **9b**)
(c) black form on white ground (Fig. **9c**)
(d) black form on black ground (Fig. **9d**)

In (a), the design is all white, and the form disappears. In (b), we have a negative form. In (c), we have a positive form. In (d), the design is all black, and the form disappears in the same way as in (a). Of course, we can have the form outlined in black in (a), and outlined in white in (d). (Fig. **10**)

If the design increases in complexity, the different possibilities for color distribution will also be increased. To illustrate once again, we have two circles crossing over each other within a frame. In the previous example, we have only two defined areas where we can distribute our colors. Now we have four areas. Still using black and white, we can present sixteen distinct variations instead of only four. (Fig. **11**)

The Interrelationships of Forms

Forms can encounter one another in numerous ways. We have just demonstrated that when one form crosses over another, the results are not as simple as we may have thought.

We now again take two circles and see how they can be brought together. We choose two circles of the same size to avoid unnecessary complication. Eight different ways of interrelationship can be distinguished:

(a) **Detachment** — The two forms remain separate from each other although they may be very close together. (Fig. **12a**)

(b) **Touching** — If we move the two forms closer, they begin to touch. The continuous

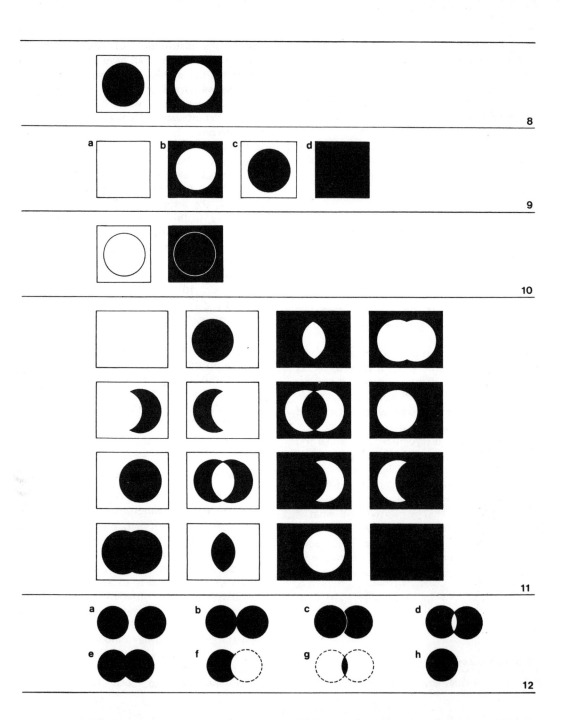

a b c d

e f g h

space which keeps the two forms apart in (a) is thus broken. (Fig. **12b**)

(c) **Overlapping** — If we move the two forms still closer, one crosses over the other and appears to remain above, covering a portion of the form that appears to be underneath. (Fig. **12c**)

(d) **Penetration** — Same as (c), but both forms appear transparent. There is no obvious above-and-below relationship between them, and the contours of both forms remain entirely visible. (Fig. **12d**)

(e) **Union** — Same as (c), but the two forms are joined together and become a new, bigger form. Both forms lose one part of their contours when they are in union. (Fig. **12e**)

(f) **Subtraction** — When an invisible form crosses over a visible form, the result is subtraction. The portion of the visible form that is covered up by the invisible form becomes invisible also. Subtraction may be regarded as the overlapping of a negative form on a positive form. (Fig. **12f**)

(g) **Intersection** — Same as (d), but only the portion where the two forms cross over each other is visible. A new, smaller form emerges as a result of intersection. It may not remind us of the orginal forms from which it is created. (Fig. **12g**)

(h) **Coinciding** — If we move the two forms still closer, they coincide. The two circles become one. (Fig. **12h**)

The various kinds of interrelationships should always be explored when forms are organized in a design.

Spatial Effects in Form Interrelationships

Detachment, touching, overlapping, penetration, union, subtraction, intersection, or coinciding of forms — each kind of interrelationship produces different spatial effects.

In detachment, both forms may appear equidistant from the eye, or one closer, one farther away.

In touching, the spatial situation of the two forms is also flexible as in detachment. Color plays an important role in determining the spatial situation.

In overlapping, it is obvious that one form is in front of or above the other.

In penetration, the spatial situation is a bit vague, but it is possible to bring one form above the other by manipulating the colors.

In union, usually the forms appear equidistant from the eye because they become one new form.

In subtraction, as well as in penetration, we are confronted with one new form. No spatial variation is possible.

In coinciding, we have only one form if the two forms are identical in shape, size, and direction. If one is smaller in size or different in shape and/or direction from the other, there will not be any real coinciding, and overlapping, penetration, union, subtraction, or intersection would occur, with the possible spatial effects just mentioned.

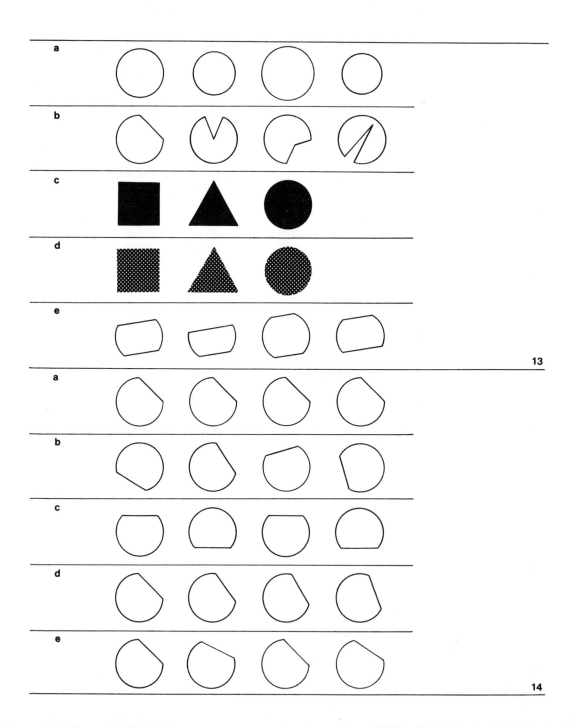

CHAPTER 3: REPETITION

Unit Forms

When a design is composed of a number of forms, those that are of identical or similar shapes are "unit forms" which appear more than once in the design.

The presence of unit forms helps to unify the design. Unit forms can be easily discovered in most designs if we search for them. A design may contain more than just one set of unit forms.

Unit forms should be simple. Overly complicated unit forms often tend to stand out too much as individual forms, and the effect of unity may be destroyed.

Repetition of Unit Forms

If we use the same form more than once in a design, we use it in repetition.

Repetition is the simplest method in designing. Columns and windows in architecture, the legs of a piece of furniture, the pattern on fabrics, tiles on the floor are obvious examples of repetition.

Repetition of unit forms usually conveys an immediate sense of harmony. Each repetitive unit form is like the beat of some kind of rhythm. When the unit forms are used in larger size and smaller numbers, the design may appear simple and bold; when they are infinitely small and in countless numbers, the design may appear to be a piece of uniform texture, composed of tiny elements.

Types of Repetition

In precise thinking, repetition should be considered in respect of each of the visual and relational elements:

(a) **Repetition of shape** — Shape is always the most important element. Repetitive shapes can have different sizes, colors, etc. (Fig. **13a**)

(b) **Repetition of size** — Repetition of size is possible only when the shapes are also repetitive or very similar. (Fig. **13b**)

(c) **Repetition of color** — This means that all the forms are of the same color but their shapes and sizes may vary. (Fig. **13c**)

(d) **Repetition of texture** — All forms can be of the same texture but they may be of different shapes, sizes, or colors. In printing, all solidly printed forms with the same type of ink on the same surface are regarded as having the same texture. (Fig. **13d**)

(e) **Repetition of direction** — This is possible only when the forms show a definite sense of direction without the slightest ambiguity. (Fig. **13e**)

(f) **Repetition of position** — This has to do with how forms are arranged in connection with the structure which will be discussed in the next chapter.

(g) **Repetition of space** — All forms can occupy space in the same manner. In other words, they may be all positive, or all negative, or related to the picture plane in the same way.

(h) **Repetition of gravity** — Gravity is too abstract an element to be used repetitively. It is difficult to say that forms are of equal heaviness or lightness, stability or instability, unless all other elements are in strict repetition.

Variations in Repetition

Repetition of all the elements may seem monotonous. Repetition of one element alone may not provoke the sense of order and harmony which we normally associate with the repetition discipline. If most of the visual elements are in repetition, possibilities in directional and spatial variations should be explored.

Directional variations — With the exception of the plain circle, all forms can vary in direction to some extent. Even circles can be grouped to give a sense of direction. Several kinds of directional arrangements can be distinguished:

(a) repeated directions (Fig. **14a**)

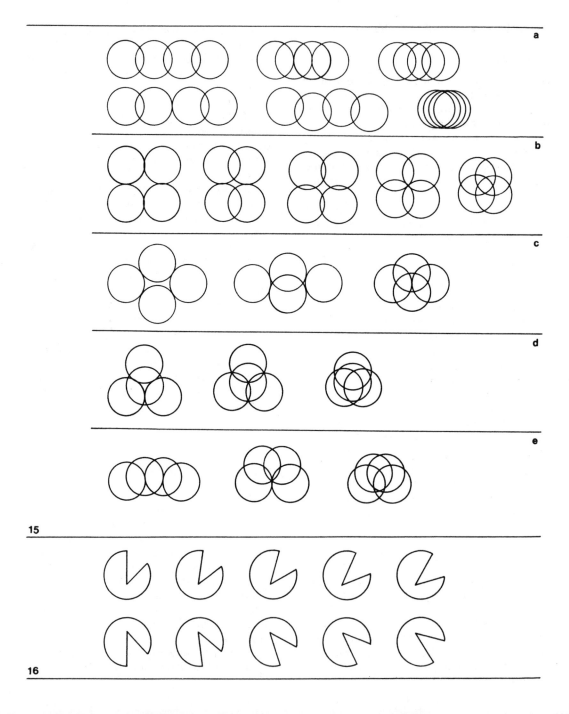

(b) indefinite directions (Fig. **14b**)

(c) alternate directions (Fig. **14c**)

(d) gradational directions (Fig. **14d**)

(e) similar directions (Fig. **14e**)

Repeated and the more regularly arranged directions can be mingled with some irregular directions.

Spatial variations — These can be obtained by having the forms encounter one another in a multiple of interrelationships as described in the previous chapter. Imaginative use of overlapping, penetration, union, or positive and negative combinations can lead to surprising results.

Sub-unit-forms and Super-unit-forms

A unit form can be composed of smaller elements that are used in repetition. Such smaller elements are called "sub-unit-forms."

If the unit forms, in the process of being organized in a design, are grouped together to become a bigger form which is then used in repetition, we call these new, bigger forms "super-unit-forms." Super-unit-forms can be used along with regular unit forms in a design if necessary.

Just as we can have more than one single type of unit form, we can have a variety of super-unit-forms if so desired.

The Encounter of Four Circles

To illustrate the formation of super-unit-forms, we will now see how four circles of the same size can be grouped together. The possibilities are definitely unlimited, but we can examine some of the common ways of arrangement as follows:

(a) **Linear arrangement** — The circles are lined up as guided by a conceptual line which passes through the centers of all the circles. The conceptual line may be straight, curved, or bent. The distance between the circles may be regulated as desired. Note, in an extreme case, that each of the circles crosses over all the other three simultaneously, producing as many as thirteen distinct divisions. (Fig. **15a**)

(b) **Square or rectangular arrangement** — In this case the four circles occupy four points which, when joined together, can form a square or a rectangle. As in (a), an extreme case also shows thirteen divisions when all the circles deeply penetrate one another. (Fig. **15b**)

(c) **Rhombic arrangement** — Here the four circles occupy four points which, when joined together, can form a rhombus. Regulating the distance between the circles, various types of super-unit-forms can emerge. (Fig. **15c**)

(d) **Triangular arrangement** — Here the four circles are arranged so that three occupy the three points of a triangle, with the fourth in the center. This also produces interesting super-unit-forms. (Fig. **15d**)

(e) **Circular arrangement** — Four circles in circular arrangement turn out the same result as in square arrangement, but circular arrangement can be very unique with more circles. Four circles can be arranged to suggest the arc of a circle, but this may be similar to a linear arrangement. (Fig. **15e**)

Repetition and Reflection

Reflection is a special case of repetition. By reflection we mean that a form is mirrored, resulting in a new form which looks very much like the original form, except that one is left-handed, and the other is right-handed, and the two can never exactly coincide.

Reflection is only possible when the form is not symmetrical, because a symmetrical form turns out to be the same form in reflection.

Rotation of a form in any direction can never produce its reflected form. The reflected form has a completely different set of rotations. (Fig. **16**)

All symmetrical forms can be divided into two parts: one component form and its reflection. The union of these two parts produces the symmetrical form.

Notes on the Exercises

Figures **17a, b, c, d, e,** and **f** all represent the results of one simple problem: repetition of unit forms (circles) of the same shape and size. There is no restriction on the number of circles used.

Figures **18a, b, c, d, e, f, g,** and **h** all represent the results of a more complex problem: students were asked to use two to four unit forms (circles) of the same shape and size to construct a super-unit-form, which is then repeated four times to make a design. Two levels of thinking are involved here. First, unit forms are not directly used to create the design but are grouped together to form super-unit-forms. Second, the super-unit-forms are used for the final design. The number of circles to be used in this problem should be no less than eight and no more than sixteen.

The results of the first problem appear to be more pleasing because there are fewer restrictions; furthermore, the students were not totally unfamiliar with some of the structures to be covered later in this book when they attempted the exercise.

The second problem is more difficult. The results, however, all demonstrate special efforts in the exploration of the various interrelationships of forms.

It is interesting to compare the results of each problem and see how much one can do with the repetition of a circle in just black and white. I should like to point out here that all the exercises illustrated in this book have been done in black and white without any intermediate gray tones. This may impose much limitation but may help the beginner to gain a thorough understanding of black and white relationships which are so essential in all design jobs requiring the technology of printing.

17

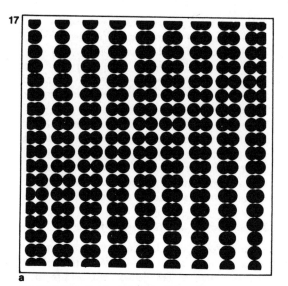

a

b

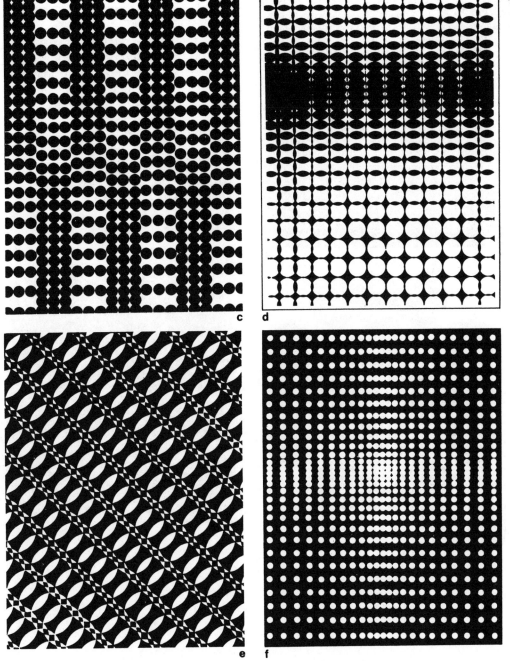

c d

e f

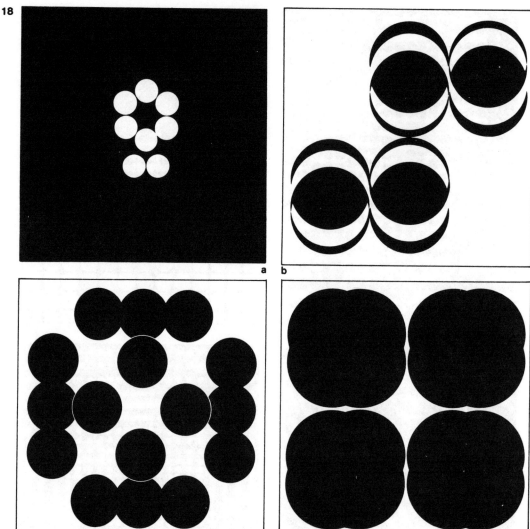

e f

g h

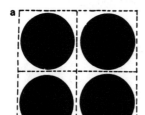

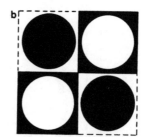

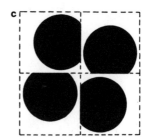

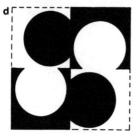

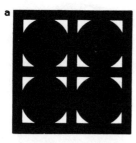

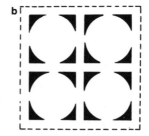

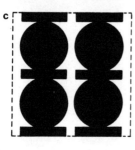

CHAPTER 4: STRUCTURE

Most designs have a structure. Structure is to govern the positioning of forms in a design. Why is one group of unit forms displayed in a row and equidistant from one another? Why does another group of unit forms suggest a circular pattern? Structure is the underlying discipline for such arrangements.

Structure generally imposes order and predetermines internal relationships of forms in a design. We may have created a design without consciously thinking of structure, but structure is always present when there is organization.

Structure can be formal, semi-formal, or informal. It can be active or inactive. It can also be visible or invisible.

Formal Structure

A formal structure consists of structural lines which are constructed in a rigid, mathematical manner. The structural lines are to guide the entire formation of the design. Space is divided into a number of subdivisions equally or rhythmically, and forms are organized with a strong sense of regularity.

The various types of formal structure are repetition, gradation, and radiation. Repetition structures will be discussed later in this chapter. The other two types of formal structure will be dealt with in Chapters 6 and 7.

Semi-formal Structure

A semi-formal structure is usually quite regular, but slight irregularity exists. It may or may not consist of structural lines to determine the arrangement of unit forms. Semi-formal structures will be discussed in Chapters 5, 8, and 10.

Informal Structure

An informal structure does not normally have structural lines. Organization is generally free and indefinite. We will come to this type of

structure when we discuss contrast in Chapter 9. It will also be touched upon in Chapter 10.

Inactive Structure

All types of structure can be active or inactive.

An inactive structure consists of structural lines which are purely conceptual. Such structural lines are constructed in a design to guide the placement of forms or unit forms, but they never interfere with their shapes nor divide the space up into distinct areas where color variations can be introduced. (Fig. 19a)

Active Structure

An active structure consists of structural lines which are also conceptual. However, the active structural lines can divide the space up into individual subdivisions which interact with unit forms they contain in various ways:

(a) The structural subdivisions provide complete spatial independence for the unit forms. Each unit form exists in isolation, as if it had its own small framal reference. It can have a ground of different color from that of its neighboring unit forms. Alternate, systematic, or random play of positive and negative forms can be introduced effectively. (Fig. **19b**)

(b) Within the structural subdivision, each unit form can move to assume various off-center positions. It can even slide partially beyond the area defined by the structural subdivision. When this happens, the portion of the unit form that is outside the confines as clearly marked by the active structural lines may be cut off. Thus, the shape of the unit form is affected. (Fig. **19c**)

(c) When the unit form intrudes into the dominion of an adjacent structural subdivision, this situation can be regarded as the encounter of two forms (the unit form and its adjacent structural subdivision), and penetration, union, subtraction, or intersection can take place as desired. (Fig. **19d**)

(d) Space isolated by a unit form in a structural subdivision can be united with any

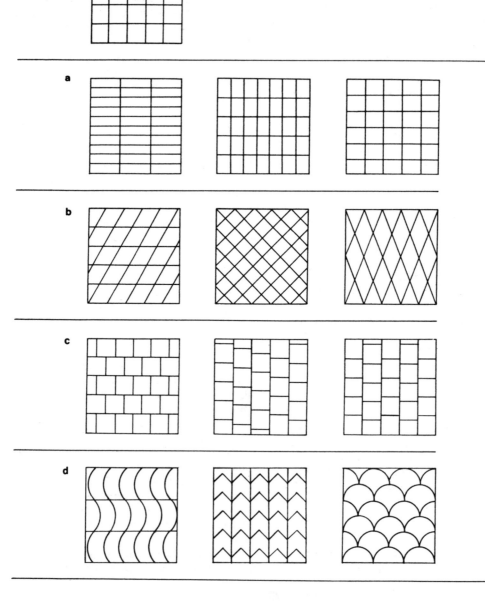

unit form or structural subdivision nearby. (Fig. 19e)

Invisible Structure

In most cases, structures are invisible, whether formal, semi-formal, informal, active, or inactive. In invisible structures, structural lines are conceptual, even though they may slice a piece off from a unit form. Such lines are active but not visible lines of measurable thickness.

Visible Structure

Sometimes a designer may prefer a visible structure. This means that the structural lines exist as actual and visible lines of desired thickness. Such lines should be treated as a special kind of unit form because they possess all the visible elements and can interact with the unit forms and the space contained by each of the structural subdivisions. (Fig. 20a)

Visible structural lines can be positive or negative. When negative, they are united with negative space or negative unit forms, and they can cross over positive space or positive unit forms. Negative structural lines are considered as visible because they have a definite thickness which can be seen and measured. (Fig. 20b)

Positive and negative visible structural lines can be used in combination in a design. For example, all horizontal structural lines can be positive, and all vertical structural lines negative. (Fig. 20c)

Visible and invisible structural lines can also be used together. This means we can have only the verticals or the horizontals visible. Or visible and invisible structural lines can be used alternately or systematically, so that the visible structural lines mark off divisions, each of which actually contains more than one regular structural subdivision. (Fig. 20d)

Repetition Structure

When unit forms are positioned regularly, with an equal amount of space surrounding each of them, they may be said to be in a "repetition structure."

A repetition structure is formal, and can be active or inactive, visible or invisible. In this type of structure, the entire area of the design (or a desired portion of it) is divided into structural subdivisions of exactly the same shape and size, without odd spatial gaps left between them.

The repetition structure is the simplest of all structures. It is particularly useful in the construction of all-over patterns.

The Basic Grid

The basic grid is the most frequently used in repetition structures. It consists of equally spaced vertical and horizontal lines crossing over each other, resulting in a number of square subdivisions of the same size. (Fig. 21)

The basic grid provides each unit form the same amount of space above, below, left, and right. Except for the direction generated by the unit forms themselves, the vertical and horizontal directions are well-balanced, with no obvious dominance of one direction over the other.

Variations of the Basic Grid

There are many other types of repetition structures, usually derived from the basic grid. Such variations of the basic grid are suggested as follows:

(a) **Change of proportion** — The square subdivisions of the basic grid can be changed into rectangular ones. The balance of the vertical and the horizontal directions is thus transformed, and one direction gains greater emphasis. (Fig. 22a)

(b) **Change of direction** — All the vertical or horizontal lines, or both, can be tilted to any angle. Such diversion from the original vertical-horizontal stability can provoke a sense of movement. (Fig. 22b)

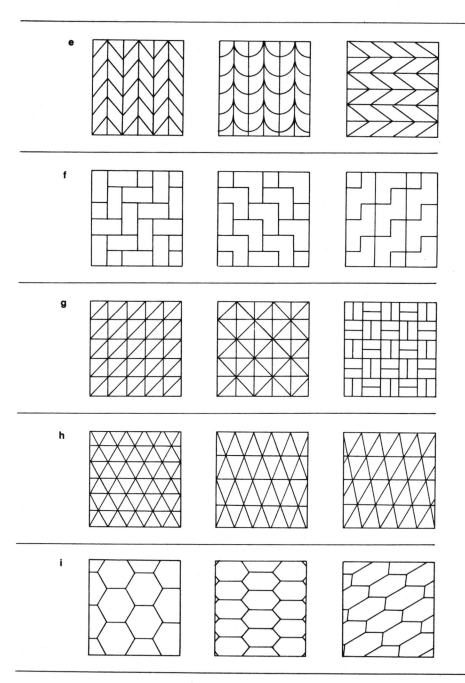

(c) **Sliding** — Each row of structural subdivisions can slide in either direction regularly or irregularly. In this case, one subdivision may not be directly above or next to another subdivision in an adjacent row. (Fig. **22c**)

(d) **Curving and/or bending** — The entire set of vertical or horizontal lines, or both, can be curved and/or bent regularly, resulting in structural subdivisions still of the same shape and size. (Fig. **22d**)

(e) **Reflecting** — A row of structural subdivisions as in (b) or (d) (provided that the two outer edges of the row are still straight and parallel to each other) can be reflected and repeated alternately or regularly. (Fig. **22e**)

(f) **Combining** — Structural subdivisions in a repetition structure can be combined to form bigger or perhaps more complex shapes. The new, bigger subdivisions should, of course, be of the same shape and size, and fit together perfectly without gaps in the design. (Fig. **22f**)

(g) **Further dividing** — Structural subdivisions in a repetition structure can be further divided into small or perhaps more complex shapes. The new, smaller subdivisions should, again, be of the same shape and size. (Fig. **22g**)

(h) **The triangular grid** — Tilting of the direction of structural lines and further dividing the subdivisions thus formed, we can obtain a triangular grid. Three well-balanced directions are usually distinguished in this triangular grid, although one or two of the directions may appear to be more prominent. (Fig. **22h**)

(i) **The hexagonal grid** — Combining six adjacent spatial units of a triangular grid produces a hexagonal grid. It can be elongated, compressed, or distorted. (Fig. **22i**)

It is necessary to note that inactive (and invisible) structures should be rather simple, because the shape of the subdivisions remains unseen. Active (both visible or invisible) structures can be more complex. Since the shape of the subdivisions is to affect the design, care should be taken in relating them to the unit forms.

Multiple Repetition Structures

When the structure consists of more than one kind of structural subdivisions which repeat both in shape and size, it is no longer a repetition structure but a "multiple repetition structure."

A multiple repetition structure is still a formal structure. The various kinds (usually two, but there can be more) of structural subdivisions are woven together in a regular pattern. Examples of this type of structure are mathematical semi-regular plane tessellations and structures consisting of repetitive shapes with regular gaps. (Fig. **23**)

Unit Forms and Structural Subdivisions

In an inactive (and invisible) structure, unit forms are either positioned in the center of structural subdivisions, or at intersections of structural lines. They can fit exactly, be smaller or bigger than the subdivisions. If bigger, adjacent unit forms will touch, overlap, penetrate, unite, subtract, or intersect one another. Sometimes they can be so big that one can cross over several others simultaneously.

In an active (visible or invisible) structure, each unit form is confined to its own spatial subdivision, but it is not necessarily placed right in the center of the subdivision. It can just fit, be smaller or bigger than the subdivision, but it is seldom so big that it extends too much beyond the area of the subdivision. Variations of position and direction can occur.

Super-unit-forms are related to the structural subdivisions in the same way, except that we may contain them in super-structural-subdivisions which consist of several regular subdivisions joined together.

Repetition of Position

This has been mentioned in the preceding chapter. Repetition of position means that the

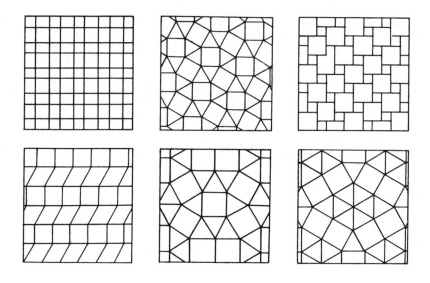

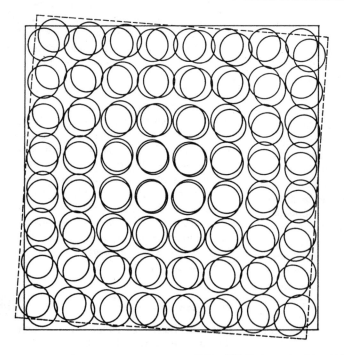

unit forms are all positioned inside each sub- division in exactly the same way.

In an inactive (and invisible) structure, there is always a repetition of position, because if the positioning of unit forms inside each subdivision varies, the regularity of the repetition structure may be easily destroyed.

In an active (visible or invisible) structure, repetition of position is not always necessary. The active or visible structural lines provide sufficient discipline of repetition so that the freedom of positioning the unit forms, plus directional variations, may be fully explored.

Superimposition of Repetition Structures

One repetition structure, along with the unit forms it carries, can be superimposed upon another repetition structure. The two structures and their unit forms can be the same or different from each other. Interaction of the two structures may produce unexpected results. (Fig. 24)

Notes on the Exercises

Figures 25a, b, c, d, e, and f exemplify the use of repetitive unit forms in an inactive (and invisible) repetition structure. The unit form here is a smaller circle enclosed by a bigger circle. The relationship of the smaller circle and the bigger circle has to remain consistent within each design.

The use of active (and invisible) repetition structures is demonstrated in figures 26a, b, c, d, e, and f. The unit form here is similar to the one used in our problem for inactive repetition structure, except that the ringlike shape is broken, suggesting a form very much like the letter C.

Comparing the results of the two problems, we should easily notice that straight lines are present in the designs with active structures but absent in those with inactive structures. The straight, active structural lines not only affect the shape of unit forms and space surrounding them, but also change the nature of the design.

a

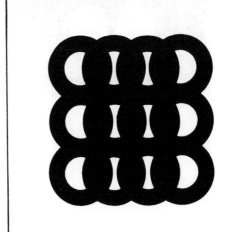

b

c | d

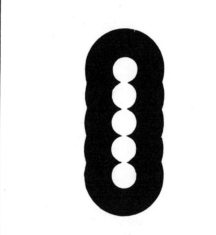

e | f

a

b

c

d

e

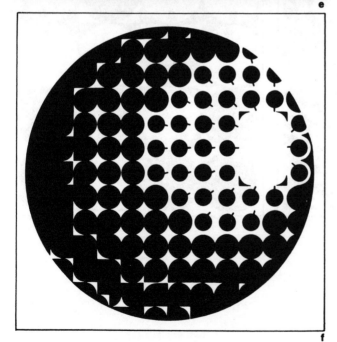

f

CHAPTER 5: SIMILARITY

Forms can resemble each other yet not be identical. If they are not identical, they are not in repetition. They are in similarity.

Aspects of similarity can be easily found in nature. The leaves of a tree, the trees in a forest, the grains of sand on a beach, the waves of the ocean are vivid examples.

Similarity does not have the strict regularity of repetition, but it still maintains the feeling of regularity to a considerable extent.

Similarity of Unit Forms

Similarity of unit forms in a design usually refers to, primarily, the similarity of shapes of unit forms. Inside a repetition structure, the sizes of unit forms have to be similar as well.

As in the case of repetition, similarity should be considered separately in respect of each of the visual and relational elements. Shape is always the main element in establishing a relationship of similarity, because forms can hardly be regarded as similar if they are similar in size, color, and texture, but different in shape.

Of course, the range of similarity of shape can be quite flexible. Shape A may look very different from shape B, but in contrast with shape C, shapes A and B can possess some relationship of similarity. Just how wide or how narrow the range of similarity should be is determined by the designer. When the range is narrow, the similar unit forms may appear to be almost repetitive. When the range is wide, the similar unit forms are seen more as individual forms, only vaguely related to one another.

Similarity of Shape

Similarity of shape does not simply mean that the forms appear more or less the same in our eyes. Sometimes similarity can be recognized when the forms all belong to a common classification. They are related to one another not so much visually as perhaps psychologically.

Similarity of shape can be created by one of the following ways:

(a) **Association** — Forms are associated with one another because they can be grouped together according to their type, their family, their meaning, or their function. The range of similarity is particularly flexible here. For instance, alphabets of one single typeface and weight definitely look alike, but we can expand the range to include all alphabets, regardless of typeface or weight. The range can still be widened as to include all forms of human writing. (Fig. 27)

(b) **Imperfection** — We can start with a shape which is regarded as our ideal shape. This ideal shape does not appear in our design, but instead we have all its imperfect variations. This can be achieved in numerous ways. The ideal shape can be disfigured, transformed, mutilated, cut up or broken up, as seen appropriate. (Fig. 28)

(c) **Spatial distortion** — A round disc, if turned in space, will appear elliptical. All forms can be rotated in the same manner, and can even be bent or twisted, resulting in a great variety of spatial distortions. (Fig. 29)

(d) **Union or subtraction** — A form can be composed of two smaller forms that are united, or obtained by subtracting a smaller form from a bigger form. The multiple ways in which the two component forms are related produce a chain of unit forms in similarity. If we allow the shapes and sizes of the component forms to vary, the range of unit forms in similarity becomes even more extensive. (Fig. 30)

(e) **Tension or compression** — A form can be stretched (by an internal force which pushes the contour outwards) or squeezed (by an external force which presses the contour inwards), resulting in a range of unit forms in similarity. This can be easily visualized if we think of the forms as something elastic, subject to tension or compression. (Fig. 31)

27

28

29

30

31

Similarity and Gradation

When a group of unit forms in similarity is used, it is essential that they should not be arranged in the design in such a way as to show a discernible systematic gradational change. As soon as the regularity of a gradational change is apparent, the effect of similarity will vanish.

Gradation is a different kind of discipline, which will be discussed in our next chapter.

Compare figures **32a** and **b**. While both use the same kind of unit forms, **32a** shows the effect of similarity, whereas **32b** shows the effect of gradation. The results are quite distinct. In similarity, the unit forms are seen in slight agitation but they stick to one another to form a unity. In gradation, the unit forms are organized to suggest progression and movement in a highly controlled manner.

The Similarity Structure

It is not easy to define a similarity structure, but we can say it is semi-formal, and does not have the rigidity of a repetition structure nor even the regularity of a multiple repetition structure.

Two basic types of similarity structure are suggested here:

Similar structural subdivisions — Structural subdivisions are not repetitive, but similar to one another. Quadrilaterals, triangles, or hexagons, all with unequal sides, can be linked together to form all-space-filling patterns. This type of structure can be active or inactive, visible or invisible. (Fig. **33**)

Visual distribution — This means that the unit forms are positioned within the framal reference of the design, visually, without the guidance of structural lines. Visual distribution in this case should allow each unit form to occupy a similar amount of space as judged by the eye. Visual distribution is related to our concept of concentration, which will be discussed in Chapter 9. (Figs. **65f** and **g**)

Notes on the Exercises

Figures **34a, b, c, d, e,** and **f** all exemplify the use of similar unit forms in a repetition structure which is active but invisible. The unit forms are based on the letter "C," just like those used for the problem on active repetition structure in Chapter 4.

If we think systematically, the unit form can be formulated as

$$A - (B + C)$$

Here A stands for the bigger circle, which is constant both in shape and size; B stands for the smaller circle, which may either be constant or variable in shape, size, and position within the bigger circle A; and C stands for the link between B and the space surrounding A, which may also be either constant or variable in shape, size, and position. Thus, a good range of unit forms in similarity can be created in this way.

By comparing the results of this problem and the active structure problem in Chapter 4, we can easily find that the discipline of similarity is more dynamic in nature than the discipline of repetition.

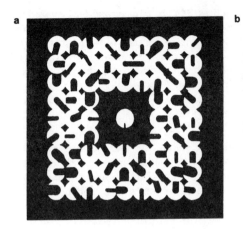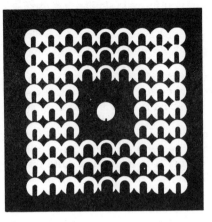

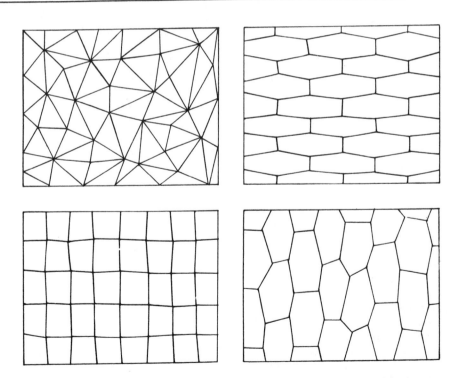

a

b

c

d

e

f

CHAPTER 6: GRADATION

We have already compared the different effects of similarity and gradation in the last chapter (figs. **32a** and **b**). Obviously gradation is a much stricter kind of discipline. It demands not just gradual change, but gradual change in an orderly way. It generates optical illusion and creates a sense of progression, which normally leads to a climax or series of climaxes.

Gradation is a daily visual experience. Things that are close to us appear large and those that are far from us appear small. If we look at a tall building with a facade of regular window patterns from a very low angle, the change in size of the windows suggests a law of gradation.

Gradation of Unit Forms

Within a repetition structure, unit forms can be used in gradation. Most visual and relational elements can be used singly or combined in gradation to achieve various effects. This means that the unit forms can have gradation of shape, size, color, texture, direction, position, space, and gravity. However, three of these elements will be dropped from our present discussion. One of these is color, which is beyond the scope of this book. The next is texture, which will be thoroughly dealt with in Chapter 11. The third is gravity, which depends on the effects produced by other elements. Eliminating these, the rest fall into three main groups: planar gradation, spatial gradation, and shape gradation.

Planar Gradation

Planar gradation does not affect the shape or the size of unit forms. The relationship between the unit forms and the picture plane always remains constant. Two kinds of planar gradation can be distinguished:

Planar rotation — This indicates the gradual change of direction of the unit forms. A shape can be rotated without diversion from the picture plane. (Fig. **35a**)

Planar progression — This indicates the gradual change of position of the unit forms within the structural subdivisions of a design. The unit forms can ascend or descend, or shift from one corner of the subdivisions to another, in a sequence of regular, gradual movements. (Fig. **35b**)

Spatial Gradation

Spatial gradation affects the shape or the size of unit forms. The relationship between the unit forms and the picture plane is never constant. Two kinds of spatial gradation can be distinguished:

Spatial rotation — With gradual diversion from the picture plane, a unit form can be rotated so that we see more and more of its edge, and less and less of its front. A flat shape can become narrower and narrower until it is almost a thin line. Spatial rotation changes the shape of a unit form. (Fig. **35c**)

Spatial progression — This is the same as the change of size. Increase or decrease of the size of unit forms suggests the forward or backward progression of unit forms in space. The unit forms are always parallel to the picture plane, but they may appear far behind the picture plane when it is small, or even in front of the picture plane when it is large. (Fig. **35d**)

Shape Gradation

This refers to the sequence of gradations which are the results of actual change of shape. Two common kinds of shape gradation are suggested:

Union or subtraction — This indicates the gradual change of positions of sub-unit-forms which make up the unit forms proper by union or subtraction. The shape and size of each of the sub-unit-forms may also undergo gradual transformations at the same time. (Fig. **35e**)

Tension or compression — This indicates the

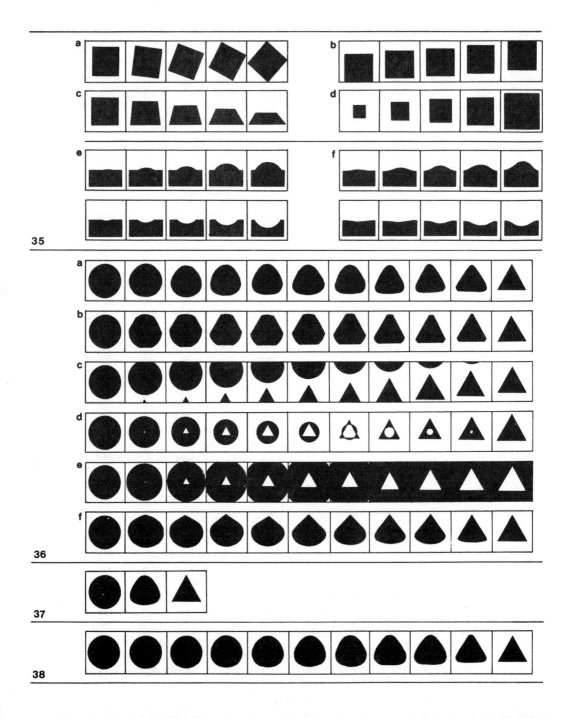

35

36

37

38

gradual change of shape of unit forms by internal or external forces. The shape appears as if it is elastic, easily affected by any slight push or pull. (Fig. 35f)

The Path of Gradation

Any form can be gradually changed to become any other form. How the change takes place is determined by the path of gradation chosen.

There are multiple paths of gradation. The designer can choose a path of planar, spatial, or shape gradation, or a combination of all these. The path can be straightforward or roundabout.

For instance, if we wish to change a circle into a triangle by shape gradation, the circle can be stretched and squeezed to become more and more triangular (fig. 36a), or it can be subtracted from three sides until it becomes a triangle (fig. 36b). By planar gradation, the circle can be shifted upwards followed by a triangle which will occupy the entire structural subdivision when the circle has completely moved out (fig. 36c). By spatial gradation, the circle can gradually diminish while the triangle can emerge simultaneously, first as a dot and then as a small triangle which gradually expands (fig. 36d). Or the circle can gradually expand beyond the confines of the structural subdivision when the triangle also emerges (fig. 36e). We can also consider the circle as the bottom of a cone which rotates to give the triangular front elevation (fig. 36f).

All the paths of gradation just described are straightforward. If a roundabout path is desired, the circle can first be changed to a square (or any other shape) before it approaches the shape of the triangle in the sequence.

The Speed of Gradation

The number of steps required for a form to change from one situation to another determines the speed of gradation. When the steps are few, the speed becomes rapid, and when the steps are many, the speed becomes slow.

The speed of gradation depends on the effects a designer wishes to achieve. A rapid gradation causes visual jerks, whereas a slow gradation evolves smoothly and sometimes almost imperceptibly. Optical illusion is usually the result of slow gradation.

It is necessary to point out that rapid gradation should be used with great caution. If a form changes too rapidly, there may not be a feeling of gradation at all, and the result may be a group of only vaguely related forms (fig. 37). Indeed we cannot change a circle effectively into a triangle in less than five steps, for normally this would require ten steps or more.

Extremely slow gradation may approach the effect of repetition, but careful arrangement of the pattern can produce very subtle results.

The speed of gradation can be changed in the middle of a sequence, or gradually quickened or slowed down for special effects. (Fig. 38)

Without alteration to the speed of gradation, a roundabout path of gradation normally takes more steps than a straightforward path.

Patterns of Gradation

In a gradation design, two factors are of importance in pattern construction: the range of gradation, and the direction of movement.

The range of gradation is marked by a starting situation and a terminating situation. In some cases, where the path of gradation is not straightforward but roundabout, intermediate situations should be taken into account. The number of steps between the starting and the terminating situations determines both the speed and the breadth of the range of gradation.

The direction of movement refers to the orientations of the starting and the terminating situations and their interrelationship. The unit forms of the starting situation can all be lined up in a row and proceed lengthwise, breadthwise, or both, with regular steps towards the terminating situation. Diagonal or other ways of progression are also possible. Some typical movement patterns in gradation are:

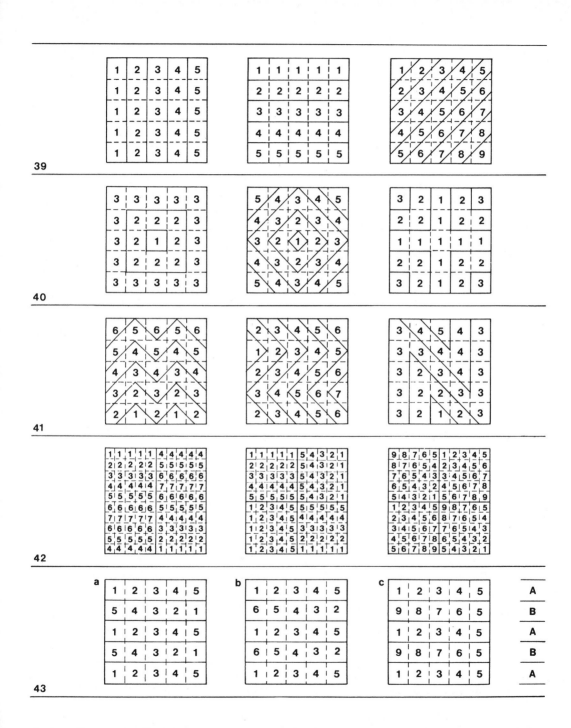

Parallel movement — This is the simplest. Unit forms are transformed gradually in parallel steps. In parallel movement, the climax is usually a straight line. (In fig. **39**, please note that the numerals signify the varying degrees of gradation and that the solid lines divide the area into zones, with each zone containing unit forms of the same step.)

Concentric movement — This means that the unit forms are transformed in concentric layers. If the starting situation is at a corner of the design, then the pattern is only partially concentric. In concentric movement, the climax may be a point, a square, or a cross. (Fig. **40**)

Zigzag movement — This means that the unit forms of the same step are arranged in a zigzag manner and are transformed at equal speed. (Fig. **41**)

In our diagrams, only twenty-five structural subdivisions (five rows of five subdivisions each) are shown. Of course, a normal gradation pattern is much bigger, and the number of steps can be extended infinitely. Also, small standardized gradation patterns may be repeated and arranged to form a bigger pattern of gradation. For example, sections of parallel movement can be joined to form a gradation design in the ways suggested in figure **42**.

It is essential to note that gradation can proceed from the starting situation to the terminating situation and then back to the starting situation with the reversal of the steps, as in the example 1-2-3-4-5-4-3-2-1. The sequence can be repeated and repeated if necessary, with smooth transitions. If regular breaks of the gradation pattern are desirable, the gradation can proceed from the starting to the terminating situation and immediately start all over again, as in 1-2-3-4-5-1-2-3-4-5.

The Gradation Structure

A gradation structure is similar to a repetition structure except that the structural subdivisions do not remain repetitive but change in size,
shape, or both, in a gradual, systematic sequence.

Most repetition structures can be converted into gradation structures. Let us examine such possibilities in the same way as we discussed the variations of the basic grid in Chapter 4:

(a) **Change of size and/or proportion** — The structural subdivisions of a basic grid can increase or decrease in size (with or without change of proportion) gradually from one to the next. The vertical or horizontal structural lines or both of the basic grid can be spaced with gradually increasing or decreasing widths. Gradation can proceed from narrow to wide, and then wide to narrow again, or can be arranged in any rhythmical sequence. (Fig. **44a**)

(b) **Change of direction** — The entire set of vertical or horizontal structural lines, or both, in (a) can be tilted in any desired direction. (Fig. **44b**)

(c) **Sliding** — The entire row of vertical or horizontal structural subdivisions in (a) or (b) can be made to slide regularly so that one subdivision is not directly next to or above another. (Fig. **44c**)

(d) **Curving, bending** — The entire set of vertical or horizontal structural lines, or both, in (a), (b), or (c) can be curved or bent gradually or regularly. (Fig. **44d**)

(e) **Reflecting** — A row of non-right-angled structural subdivisions as in (b) or (d) can be reflected and repeated alternately or regularly. (Fig. **44e**)

(f) **Combining** — Structural subdivisions in (a) or (b) can be combined to form bigger or more complex shapes with the effect of gradation. (Fig. **44f**)

(g) **Further dividing** — Structural subdivisions in all gradation structures can be subdivided into smaller or more complex shapes. (Fig. **44g**)

(h) **The triangular grid** — The triangular grid of a repetition structure can be transformed into a gradation structure by gradually varying the size and shape of the triangles. (Fig. **44h**)

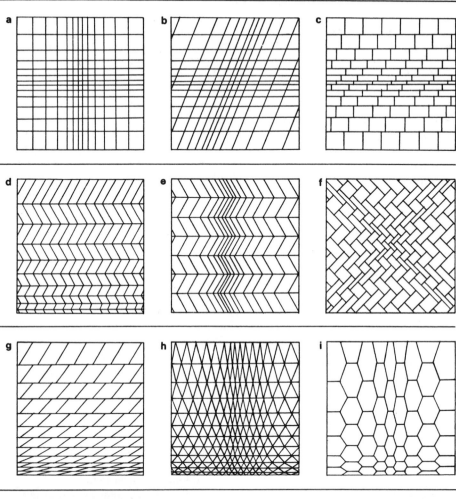

a **b** **c**

d **e** **f**

g **h** **i**

44

a

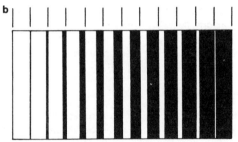

b

45

(i) **The hexagonal grid** — The hexagonal grid of a repetition structure can be transformed into a gradation structure by gradually varying the size and shape of the hexagons. (Fig. 44i)

Alternate Gradation

Alternate gradation provides unusual complexity in a gradation design. It means that gradually changing unit forms or structural subdivisions from opposite directions are interwoven together. The simplest way to achieve alternate gradation is to divide the structure (either the vertical or the horizontal rows) into odd and even rows, and have all the odd rows observe a discipline different from the even rows.

To illustrate this, we have figure **43**, in which A stands for the odd rows and B stands for the even rows. To have alternate gradation of unit forms, we can arrange in A rows unit forms to be transformed from left to right, and in B rows the exact opposite (fig. **43a** and also fig. **17c**, which is a finished design). However, it is not necessary that the steps of gradation in A and B rows should be the same. Variations of these are suggested in figures **43b** and **c**. Manipulating the range, speed, and direction of gradation, we can have almost unlimited kinds of variation. Unit forms, if they are not used gradationally in both A and B rows, can be used gradationally in one set of the rows, and repetitively (in straight or alternate repetition) in the other set of rows.

If the unit forms are in gradation of size, the space left over by diminishing unit forms can be used for the accommodation of a set of unit forms in reverse gradation. Here the original unit forms can occupy the central portion of the structural subdivisions, whereas a new set of unit forms can occupy intersections of the structural lines. (Fig. **45a**)

In a gradation structure, alternate gradation can be obtained if the A rows gradually diminish while the B rows gradually expand simultaneously in the same direction. This is illustrated in figure **45b** with black bands standing for the A rows and white bands for the B rows. The illustration may look rather complicated, but the method of construction can be very simple. The combined width of every pair of A and B rows should always remain constant (or in very slow gradation). Thus we can first divide the entire width of the design area into combined rows of A+B, and then we can further divide each of the combined rows into an A row and a B row, carefully allowing A to expand step by step from one combined row to the next. Since the width of the combined row is constant, if A expands, B automatically contracts.

Relationship of Unit Forms and Structures in a Gradation Design

A gradation design can be obtained in one of the following ways: gradational unit forms in a repetition structure; repetitive unit forms in a gradation structure; and gradational unit forms in a gradation structure.

It should be noted that either the unit forms or the structure or both could be in gradation. A repetition structure is flexible enough to contain most kinds of gradational unit forms, whereas a gradation structure may have many restrictions.

In a gradation structure, the structural subdivisions can range from very big to very small, or very narrow to very wide. They change both in shape and size, making accommodation of more complex kinds of unit form difficult.

Notes on the Exercises

Figures **46a, b, c,** and **d** exemplify the use of gradational unit forms (circles in this case) in a repetition structure. Compare these with figures **17d** and **f**, which feature repeated circles in a gradation structure. Figures **47a** through **h** exemplify the use of gradational unit forms (in this case a stylized alphabet) in a gradation structure. While the latter problem represents a new departure, the former is closely linked with all the problems in preceding chapters, with the circle as a recurring motif.

a
b
c
d

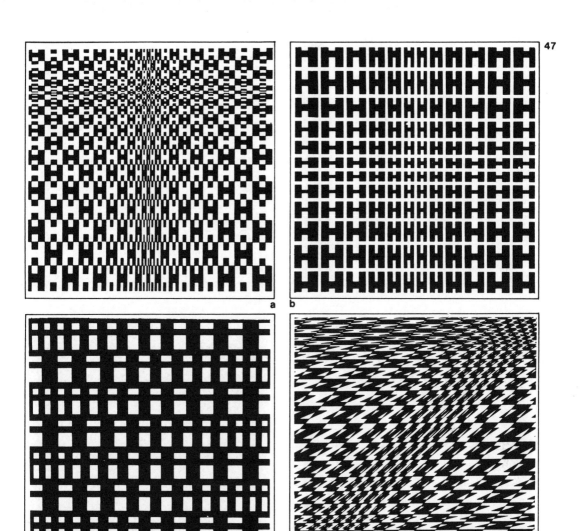

a b

c d

47

e f

g h

CHAPTER 7: RADIATION

Radiation may be described as a special case of repetition. Repeated unit forms or structural subdivisions which revolve regularly around a common center produce a pattern of radiation.

Radiation is a common phenomenon in nature. Look at the flowers in bloom and you can always discover radiation patterns in the arrangements of their petals. Dropping a stone on calm waters generates concentric ripples, which also suggest a kind of radiation. In an abstract way, the sun radiates light rays; so do most luminous objects.

Radiation can have the effect of optical vibration that we find in gradation. The repetition of unit forms or structural subdivisions around a common center has to go through a gradation of directions. Therefore, radiation may also be called a special case of gradation. Sometimes the division between a gradation pattern and a radiation pattern is rather vague, as in the case when the climax of a gradation pattern is located in the center.

A radiation pattern arrests the attention immediately. It is very useful when a powerful, eye-catching design is required.

Characteristics of a Radiation Pattern

A radiation pattern has the following characteristics, which help to distinguish it from a repetition or gradation pattern:

(a) It is generally multi-symmetrical.

(b) It has a very strong focal point, which is usually located at the center of the design.

(c) It can generate optical energy and movement from or towards the center.

The Radiation Structure

A radiation structure consists of two important factors, the interplay of which establishes all the variations and complexity:

Center of radiation — This marks the focal point around which unit forms are positioned.

It should be noted that the center of radiation is not always the physical center of the design.

Directions of radiation — This refers to the directions of structural lines as well as the directions of the unit forms.

For the sake of convenience, three main kinds of radiation structure may be distinguished: centrifugal, concentric, and centripetal. Actually, the three are very much interdependent. The centrifugal radiation structure may require a concentric structure to help in the placement of its unit forms. The centripetal usually needs a centrifugal structure to guide its construction. The concentric must have a centrifugal structure to determine its structural subdivisions.

The Centrifugal Structure

This is the commonest kind of radiation structure. In it, structural lines radiate regularly from the center or its vicinity in all directions.

(a) **The basic centrifugal structure** — This consists of straight structural lines radiating from the center of the pattern. All the angles formed by the structural lines at the center should be equal. (Fig. **48a**)

(b) **Curving or bending of structural lines** — The straight structural lines in (a) can be curved or bent regularly as desired. When bending occurs, the positions where the structural lines start to make an abrupt turn are determined by a shape (usually a circle, the center of which coincides with the center of the radiation pattern) which is superimposed upon the structural lines. (Fig. **48b**)

(c) **Center of radiation in off-center position** — The center of radiation is often also the physical center of the design, but it can be placed in an off-center position, as far as the edge or even beyond it. (Fig. **48c**)

(d) **Opening up of the center of radiation** — The center of radiation can be opened up to form a round, oval, triangular, square, or polygonal hole. In this case, the structural lines do not radiate from the center of the hole but

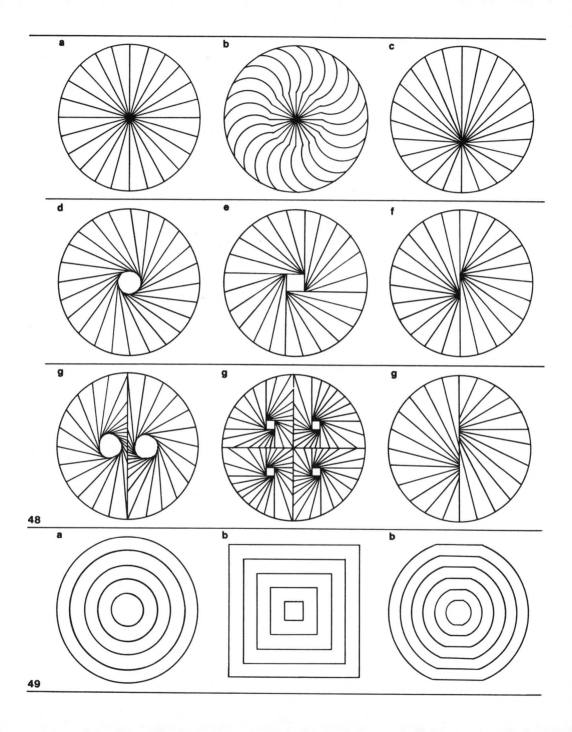

a

b

c

d

e

f

g

g

g

48

a

b

b

49

run as tangents to the circular hole or as extensions of the sides of the central triangle, square, or polygon. (Fig. **48d**)

(e) **Multiple centers, by opening up of the center of radiation** — After the center of radiation has been opened up and a regular triangle, square, or polygon appears, each vertex of the triangle, square, or polygon can become a center of radiation. This means that if the polygon is a hexagon, there will be six centers of radiation. The design is divided into six sectors, with each sector its own center of radiation from which structural lines are radiated. (Fig. **48e**)

(f) **Multiple centers, by splitting and sliding the center of radiation** — A center of radiation can be split into two by having half of the design radiate from one off-center position, and the remaining half from another off-center position, with the two centers on one straight line which passes through the physical center of the design. More centers can be created in similar fashion. (Fig. **48f**)

(g) **Multiple centers or hidden multiple centers, by combining sections of off-center radiation structures** — Two or more sections of off-center radiation structures can be organized and combined to form a new radiation structure. The result is a multiple-center radiation whether the centers are visible or hidden. (Fig. **48g**)

The Concentric Structure

In a concentric structure, instead of radiating from the center as in a centrifugal structure, structural lines surround the center in regular layers.

(a) **The basic concentric structure** — This consists of layers of equally spaced circles enclosing the center of the design which is also the common center of all the circles. (Fig. **49a**)

(b) **Straightening, curving, or bending of structural lines** — The concentric structural lines as in (a) can be straightened, curved, or bent regularly, as desired. In fact, any single shape can be made into concentric layers. (Fig. **49b**)

(c) **Shifting of centers** — Instead of having a common center, the circles can shift their centers along the track of a line, which may be straight, curved, bent, and possibly forming a circle, triangle, square, or any desired shape. Usually swirling movements result. (Fig. **49c**)

(d) **The spiral** — A geometrically perfect spiral is very difficult to construct. However, a less perfect but still regular spiral can be obtained by dissecting the basic concentric structure and putting the sectors back again. Shifting of centers and adjusting of the radii of the circles can also produce a spiral. A spiral pattern generates strong centrifugal force, so it is halfway between a centrifugal and a concentric structure. (Fig. **49d**)

(e) **Multiple centers** — By taking a section or a sector of a concentric structure and repeating it, sometimes with necessary adjustments, a concentric structure with multiple centers can be constructed. (Fig. **49e**)

(f) **Distorted and/or hidden centers** — This can be created in the same way as described in (e), but instead of resulting in multiple centers, the design may contain a distorted center, or several hidden centers. (Fig. **49f**)

(g) **Gradual rotation of concentric layers** — If the concentric layers are not perfect circles but squares, polygons, or irregular shapes, they can be gradually rotated. (Fig. **49g**)

(h) **Concentric layers with centrifugal radiations** — Centrifugal radiations can be constructed within each concentric layer. (Fig. **49h**)

(i) **Reorganized concentric layers** — The concentric layers can be reorganized so that some of the structural lines can be bent and linked with other structural lines, resulting in interwoven patterns with one or more centers. (Fig. **49i**)

The Centripetal Structure

In this kind of structure, sequences of bent or curved structural lines press towards the center.

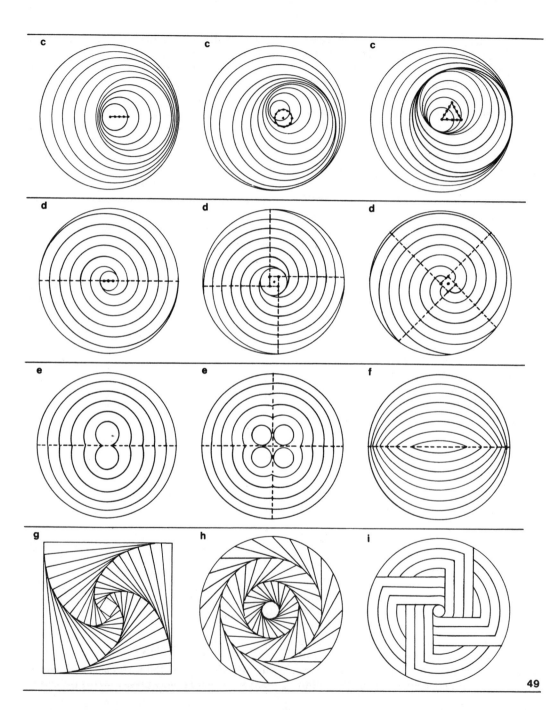

d d d

e e f

g h i

The center is not where all the structural lines will converge but where all angles or curves formed by the structural lines point towards.

(a) **The basic centripetal structure** — This consists of equal sectors within each of which are constructed equidistant lines parallel to the two straight sides of the sector, forming a series of angles progressing towards the center. (Fig. **50a**)

(b) **Directional change of structural lines** — The parallel lines in the basic centripetal structure can change in direction, so that increasingly acute or obtuse angles are formed at the joining points of the structural lines. (Fig. **50b**)

(c) **Curving and bending of structural lines** — The structural lines can be curved or bent regularly, creating complex changes within the pattern. (Fig. **50c**)

(d) **Opening up of the center of radiation** — By sliding the sectors of a centripetal structure, the center of radiation can be opened up and a triangle, square, polygon, or starshape can be formed. (Fig. **50d**)

Superimposition of Radiation Structures

As pointed out earlier, the three kinds of radiation structure are interdependent. Unless the unit forms are just the structural lines themselves made visible, each kind of radiation structure generally requires another to produce fine structural subdivisions for the accommodation of unit forms. (Fig. **51a**)

Superimposition in this way is just a practical necessity. Which kind of radiaiton structure will dominate during this superimposition depends on the shape and positioning of the unit forms.

Sometimes one radiation structure is superimposed upon another of the same type or a different type with a different purpose. The result is a complex composition, often producing interesting moiré patterns. (Fig. **51b**)

Radiation and Repetition

A radiation structure may sometimes be superimposed upon a repetition structure. With the repetition structure remaining unchanged, the radiative structural lines may be shifted slightly so that the continuity of the radiative lines from one repetitive structural subdivision to the next is interrupted to provoke a sense of movement. (Figs. **52a** and **b**)

A radiation structure may also be superimposed upon simple repetitive forms guided by an inactive repetition structure. (Fig. **52c**)

Radiation and Gradation

Most of the radiation structures illustrated earlier in this chapter are constructed with repetitive angles and/or spacing. However, gradational angles and/or spacing may be used in a great many of the cases. (Figs. **55f** and **g**)

A radiation structure may be superimposed on a gradation structure or a group of gradational unit forms in the same way as it is superimposed on a repetition structure or a group of repetitive forms.

Structural Subdivisions and Unit Forms

Structural subdivisions in a radiation structure are usually either repetitive or gradational, although they may also be similar to or plainly different from one another.

In a centrifugal structure, the subdivisions are generally repetitive in both shape and size. Unit forms fit these subdivisions in the same way that they fit those in a repetition structure, except that the subdivisions normally carry the unit forms in their directional rotation. The unit forms may conform to the directions of the subdivisions or maintain a constant angle to the axis of each subdivision. (Figs. **53a** and **b**)

Within each of the subdivisions in a centrifugal structure, finer subdivisions can be constructed if desired. A sequence of parallel lines can be employed for the purpose, but there is virtually no limit to the ways of making further subdivisions. (Fig. **53c**)

In a regular concentric structure, the subdivisions are in the form of a ring which can only accommodate unit forms of a linear nature.

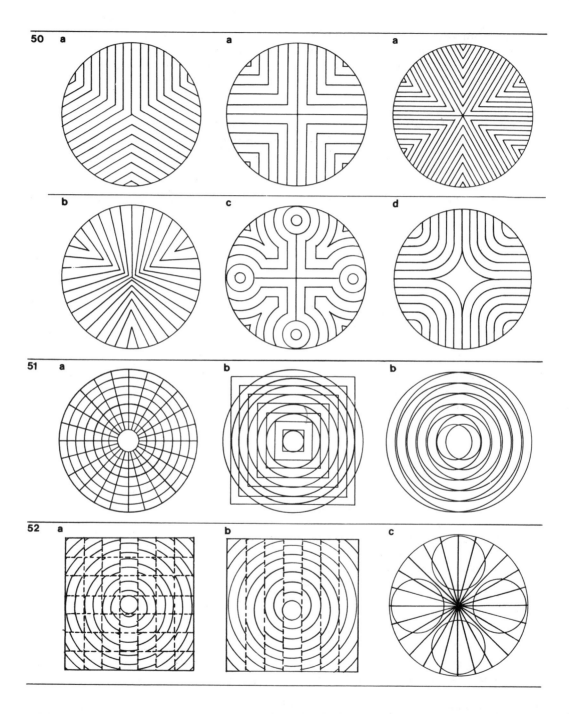

A centrifugal structure is usually required for making fine subdivisions, and each ring can be rotated variably, if necessary, so that the subdivisions in one ring do not have to align with those in the next ring.(Fig. **53d**) Subdivisions obtained in this way are generally repetitive within each ring, but gradational from the center towards outer rings. Unit forms fit these subdivisions in the same way as they fit those in a gradation structure. Of course it is also possible to subdivide each concentric ring in a different manner if desired. (Fig. **53e**)

In a regular centripetal structure, the subdivisions are defined by sets of parallel lines which curl or bend towards the center. These can be further divided by superimposing sets of parallel lines, another centripetal structure, or a concentric structure. (Figs. **53f, g, h**, and **i**)

Unit Forms in Radiation

We have spoken of unit forms in repetition, similarity, and gradation, and in each of these disciplines all the visual and relational elements can be considered. Radiation is a kind of discipline which involves structure only. If we have to speak of unit forms in radiation, it will be the concentric movement discussed under the heading of "Patterns of Gradation" in the chapter on gradation. Concentric movement creates a feeling of radiation, but basically it is a gradational use of unit forms. In planar rotation, the unit forms can be rotated in such a way that they all point to the physical center of the design. In planar progression, they can gradually move towards or away from the center from one concentric ring to the next. (Fig. **54a**)

Unit forms can be designed as miniature radiation patterns which are arranged repetitively or gradationally in a repetition structure. The effect is still very much like radiation. (Fig. **54b**)

Oversize Unit Forms

A unit form can sometimes be almost as big as the entire radiation pattern itself, or its length or breadth can be comparable to the diameter of radiation. Such oversize unit forms can be rotated along a centrifugal structure, maintaining a fixed relationship to each of the structural lines. During rotation, one unit form will inevitably cross over several or all other unit forms, and careful manipulation of overlapping, penetration, union, subtraction, and intersection will produce exciting results. (Fig. **54c**)

Irregular and Distorted Radiation

Any irregular departure from regular radiation structures can be made if desired. Irregularity can occur only in one section of a regular pattern, but the entire design can be created with a vague center and loosely scattered radiating elements or series of irregular concentric rings.

Photography and other mechanical means can be used to distort a regular radiation pattern. The pattern drawn or painted on paper can be photographed with a special lens, through a textured transparent screen or at an angle. It can also be curled, creased, folded, or crumpled, and then made into a flat picture by means of photography.

Notes on the Exercises

Figures **55a** through **n** all illustrate radiation designs with unit forms more or less of a linear nature. In some examples the unit forms are just the structural lines made visible; in other examples they are designed to fit structural subdivisions.

No attempt is made here to group the examples into the three kinds of radiation structure discussed in this chapter, because although some are immediately distinguishable as this or that kind, most are a blending of the different kinds. It is strongly suggested that the examples should be carefully analyzed.

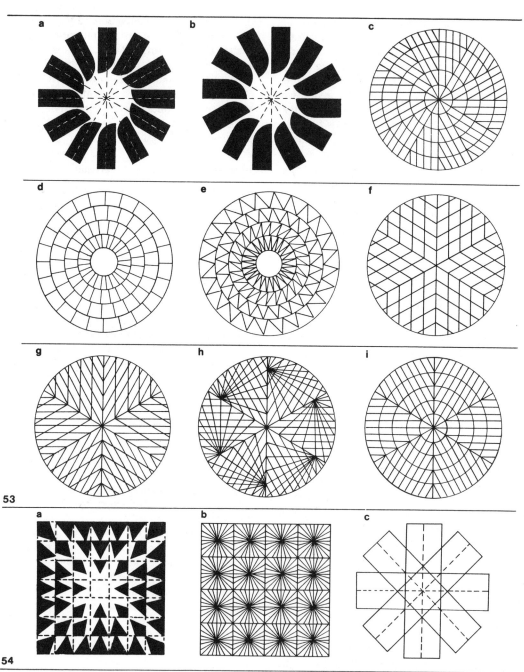

53

54

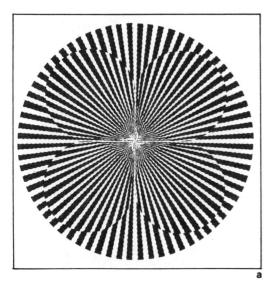

a

b

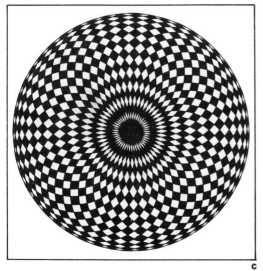

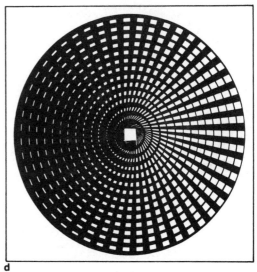

c

d

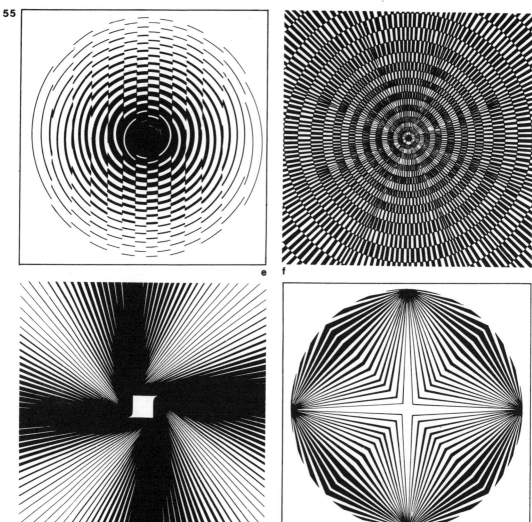

55

e f

g h

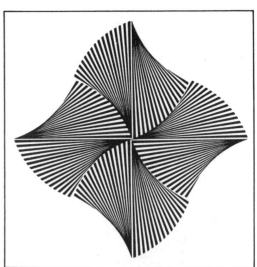

i j

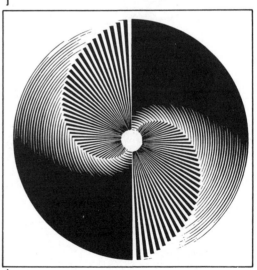

k l

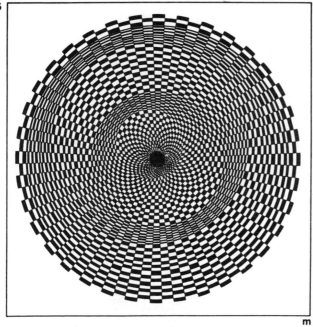

m

n

CHAPTER 8: ANOMALY

Anomaly is the presence of irregularity in a design in which regularity still prevails. It marks a certain degree of departure from the general conformity, resulting in slight or considerable interruption of the overall discipline. Sometimes anomaly is just a singular element among uniform organization.

Examples of anomaly around us are common: flowers among foliage, the moon in a starry night, cracks on a plain wall, an old church among modern skyscrapers.

In design, the use of anomaly has to be of genuine necessity. It must have a definite purpose, which may be one of the following:

(a) **To attract attention** — When anomaly is used sparingly, it tends to stand out and attract immediate attention. Center of interest can be created if anomaly happens only within a restricted area of the design.

(b) **To relieve monotony** — Plain regularity can be monotonous. Anomaly is able to generate movement and vibration. Anomalous areas in this case should be scattered either casually or systematically all over the design.

(c) **To transform regularity** — One kind of regularity can be transformed into another. Here anomaly is just a change of discipline.

(d) **To break down regularity** — Regularity can be completely broken down into disorder in one or more areas. Anomaly seems to be more violent in this case, but the unity of the design should be maintained.

These purposes will be discussed further when anomaly among unit forms and anomaly within structures are dealt with separately.

Anomaly among Unit Forms

Regularity exists among unit forms when they are related to each other under a certain kind of discipline, which may be repetition, similarity, or gradation. However, if we consider all the visual and relational elements, the relationship of various unit forms can be rather complex. Unit forms may be repetitive in all aspects, but they may also be repetitive only in certain elements and gradational in the remaining elements.

When anomaly is introduced among unit forms, the originality of each of the visual and relational elements should be carefully examined. An anomalous unit form does not have to be different in every way from the general regularity. It can deviate in just one or two elements and conform to the general regularity in all other elements.

Anomaly is comparative. One anomalous unit can be more anomalous than another. Anomaly can be so subtle that it is barely noticeable, or it can be extremely prominent. Anomalous unit forms can maintain a certain kind of regularity among themselves, or they can be quite different among themselves.

Anomalous unit forms can attract attention in one or more of the following ways: (a) the anomaly is prominent; (b) all anomalous unit forms appear within a restricted area; (c) there are only a few of these anomalous unit forms (or there is only one). Concentrated anomaly normally becomes the center of interest in a design. (Fig. **56a**)

Anomaly relieves monotony when the anomalous unit forms appear quite frequently, scattering over a wide area. They can be fairly indistinct, occurring as minor distortions or transfigurations of the regular unit forms. Their placement in the design can be orderly or casual, generating movements and adding accentuations. (Fig. **56b**)

Regularity can be transformed from one kind to another when anomalous unit forms also establish a kind of regularity among themselves. Such anomalous unit forms are not just related to each other regularly, but are also arranged regularly. This is like merging or annexing two different groups of regular unit forms. The minority group is an anomaly in terms of the

56

57

majority, but sometimes such distinction may be rather vague. (Fig. **56c**)

Regularity can be broken down when unit forms in one or more areas appear to be torn, cracked, fractured, or dissolved. This can be more effective if the structure is also disrupted. (Fig. **56d**)

Anomaly within Structures

The regular structures are those of repetition, gradation, and radiation. Similarity structures are less regular, but still maintain a certain degree of regularity.

Anomaly within a regular structure occurs when structural subdivisions in one or more areas of the design change in shape, size, or direction, become dislocated, or fall into complete disorganization. This marks one further step towards informality, but the structure is still a formal one apart from the anomalous areas.

Obviously unit forms are contained in structures of this nature. In areas where structural anomaly occurs, unit forms can be affected in one or more of the following ways:

(a) Their visual elements remain unaffected, but they may be forced to shift in position or direction, possibly crossing over adjacent structural subdivisions or unit forms.

(b) Their visual elements remain unaffected, but the anomalous structural lines, being active in this case, may trim off portions of the unit forms which are not totally confined within their respective subdivisions.

(c) They may be distorted as the subdivisions are distorted, but their relationship with the subdivisions remains consistent.

(d) They may become anomalous while maintaining a kind of regularity among themselves.

(e) They may become anomalous variously.

Structural anomaly can attract attention when it happens quite noticeably within a restricted area. Even if all the visual elements of the unit forms stay unchanged, structural anomaly stretches or squeezes space which easily draws the eye to focus on. (Fig. **57a**)

Monotony in plain regularity can be relieved with frequent occurrence of anomalous structural subdivisions distributed in an orderly way or casually all over the design. This causes interesting variations of blank space and positioning of unit forms, the shapes and/or sizes of which may or may not be affected. (Fig. **57b**)

The area or areas of anomaly may be just another kind of structural regularity different from the general discipline. Transformation of regularity can lead to exciting semi-formal compositions. (Fig. **57c**)

Breakdown in a regular structure means that discipline is completely destroyed in one or more areas of anomaly. Structural lines get entangled, subdivisions distorted or dislocated, or the structure partially disintegrates. (Fig. **57d**)

Notes on the Exercises

The uses of anomaly are shown in figures **58a, b, c, d, e, f, g, h, i,** and **j**. Unit forms in these exercises are mainly of a linear nature. There is no restriction as to how general regularity dominates the design and how anomaly is introduced. Please note the effect of anomaly in each of the examples.

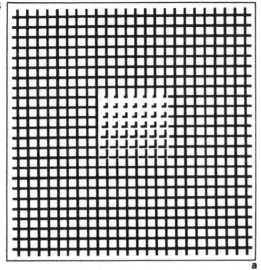

a

b

c

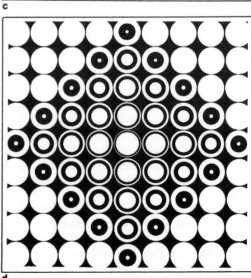

d

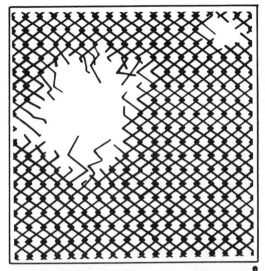

e

g

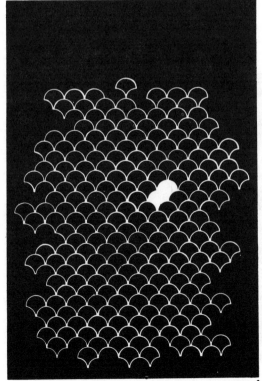

f

h

i

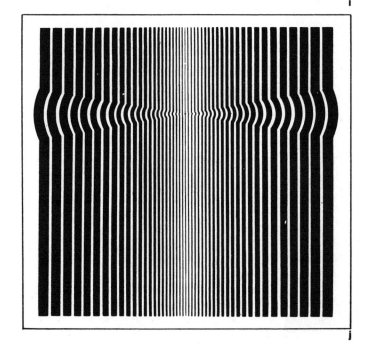

j

CHAPTER 9: CONTRAST

Contrast happens all the time, although its presence may be overlooked. There is contrast when a form is surrounded by blank space. There is contrast when a straight line meets a curve. There is contrast when one form is much bigger than another. There is contrast when vertical and horizontal directions coexist.

We experience all sorts of contrasts in our daily life. The day is in contrast with the night; a flying bird is in contrast with the sky; an old chair is in contrast with a modern sofa.

Contrast ranges far beyond commonly acknowledged opposites. It is quite flexible: it may be mild or severe, vague or obvious, simple or complex. Form A may appear contrasting to form B, but when form C is brought in, forms A and B may appear similar rather than contrasting to one another, and both of them can be contrasting to form C in varying degrees.

Contrast is just a kind of comparison whereby differences are made clear. Two forms can be found similar in certain aspects and different in other aspects. Their differences become emphasized when contrast takes place. A form may not look big when it is seen alone, but may appear gigantic against tiny forms next to it.

Contrast, Regularity, and Anomaly

Anomaly exists in regularity as irregular elements. There is contrast between anomaly and regularity because regularity is the observation of, whereas anomaly is the departure from, a certain kind of discipline. However, contrast exists also within regularity itself.

Unless the design is nothing but a solidly and uniformly colored flat surface, there is always contrast between occupied and unoccupied space. In the arrangement of unit forms which are repetitive in shape, size, color, and texture, contrasts of position and/or direction may take place. Unit forms themselves may consist of contrasting elements in one way or another. All the contrasting elements can be woven together in the design as intrinsic parts of the regularity.

Regularity does not necessarily make a good design, although it may guarantee a certain degree of harmony. The same group of unit forms used in a repetition structure can be a dull design in the hands of one designer, but an exciting design in the hands of another. Proper use of contrast in the relational elements can make the difference.

Contrast of Visual and Relational Elements

Let us examine the use of contrast in respect of each of the visual and relational elements:

(a) **Contrast of shape** — Contrast of shape is quite complicated because a shape can be described in a multiplicity of ways. There is contrast between a geometric shape and an organic one, but two geometric shapes can be in contrast if one is angular but the other non-angular. Other common cases of contrast of shape are: curvilinear/rectilinear, planar/linear, mechanical/calligraphic, symmetrical/asymmetrical, beautiful/ugly, simple/complex, abstract/representational, undistorted/distorted, etc. (Fig. **59a**)

(b) **Contrast of size** — Contrast of size is straightforward. Big/small contrast is seen among planar forms, whereas long/short contrast is seen among linear forms. (Fig. **59b**)

(c) **Contrast of color** — Detailed discussions of color contrasts are beyond the scope of the present book, but some common cases can be mentioned here: light/dark, brilliant/dull, warm/cool, etc. (Fig. **59c**)

(d) **Contrast of texture** — Texture will form the subject of a later chapter. However, some typical cases of textural contrasts are: smooth/rough, fine/coarse, even/uneven, matt/glossy, etc. (Fig. **59d**)

(e) **Contrast of direction** — Any two directions meeting each other at an angle of 90 degrees are in maximum contrast. Two forms directly facing each other create a directional

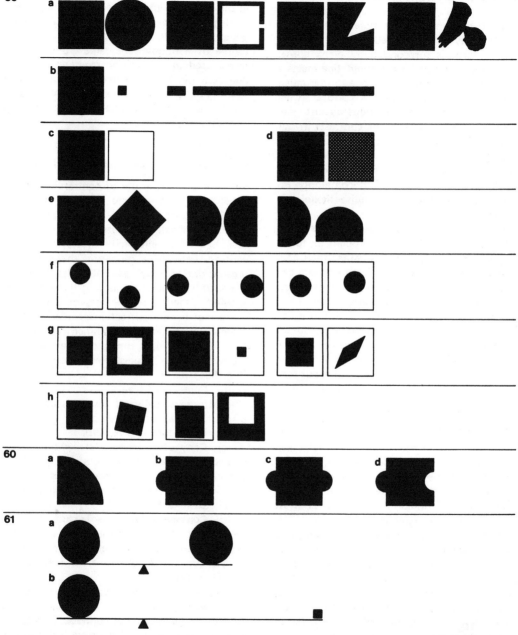

contrast of quite a different nature, because they are not unparallel, although one of them has been rotated a full 180 degrees. (Fig. 59e)

(f) **Contrast of position** — The position of a form is recognized as related to the framal reference, the center, the structural subdivision that contains it, the structural lines nearby, or another form. The common positional contrasts are: top/bottom, high/low, left/right, central/off-center. (Fig. 59f)

(g) **Contrast of space** — Space will also form the subject of a later chapter. When space is considered as a flat plane, contrasts are perceived as occupied/unoccupied or positive/negative. Blank space can be seen as congested or expansive, and can have contrasts of shape and size if it is read as a negative form. When space is considered as illusory, forms may appear to advance or recede, to be near or far, flat or three-dimensional, parallel or unparallel to the picture plane, etc., in spatial contrast with one another. (Fig. 59g)

(h) **Contrast of gravity** — There are two types of gravitational contrasts: stable/unstable and light/heavy. Stability or instability may be due to the shape itself, or due to conformity to or deviation from either verticality or horizontality. A stable form is static, whereas an unstable form suggests movement. Lightness or heaviness of a form may be due to the use of color, but is also affected by shape and size. (Fig. 59h)

Contrasts within a Form

It is common for individual forms or unit forms to contain contrasting elements which may help to make them look more interesting. Sometimes contrast exists without being noticed, but a designer should be sensitive of its presence. Effective use of contrast is of paramount importance in designing.

To sharpen our awareness of contrasts within a form, we now take four forms and examine them carefully:

Figure **60a** is composed of three edge lines, two straight lines of the same length being part of a square, and a curved line being part of a circle. There is a contrast of shape (angular/non-angular).

Figure **60b** is composed of a square and a circle. The circle is obviously much smaller than the square. So there is not just a contrast of shape (angular/non-angular), but also a contrast of size (big/small).

Figure **60c** is composed of one square and two circles. The circles are small in size, as in figure **60b**. So there is a contrast of shape as well as a contrast of size, and then there is also a contrast of position (left/right) between the two small circles.

Like figure **60c**, figure **60d** is composed of one square and two circles, but in a different way. There is a contrast of shape as well as a contrast of size and a contrast of position. Furthermore, there is a contrast of space (positive/negative), because one circle is united to the square, but the other circle is subtracted from it.

The Contrast Structure

Manipulation of contrasts of the relational elements can establish a contrast structure. This kind of structure is completely informal, with strict regularity excluded as far as possible.

As we have already seen, a formal structure (repetition, gradation, or radiation) consists of regularly constructed structural lines or subdivisions which guide the organization of unit forms into a definite order. An informal structure has no structural lines, and unit forms are positioned freely. Balance is to be maintained in both cases, but the kind of balance in each case is different. To illustrate this, balance in a formal structure is like distributing two equal weights equidistantly from the fulcrum (fig. **61a**), whereas balance in an informal structure is like distributing two unequal weights at unequal distances from the fulcrum, with the

a

b

c

d

lighter weight farther away, the heavier weight nearer by, with careful adjustments (fig. 61b).

In a contrast structure, unit forms are seldom repetitive in both shape and size but are in a loose relationship of similarity. They may have more than just one kind, but usually there is one kind that dominates. Among the two or more kinds of unit forms, contrasts of shape, size, and/or color may exist.

No definite rules can be established in the organization of a contrast structure. Shapes and sizes of unit forms are adjusted as felt necessary. Similarity is sought, not just among each of the visual elements, but among the relational elements as well in order to maintain a sense of unity, with occasional contrasts to produce tension and visual excitement.

We will now see how each relational element can be manipulated in a contrast structure:

(a) **Direction** — Most of the unit forms may have similar directions. Contrasting directions are used to provoke agitation. We can also arrange the unit forms in all sorts of directions, creating varying degrees of contrast among them. (Fig. 62a)

(b) **Position** — Unit forms can be positioned towards opposite borders of the framal reference, creating tension in between. (Fig. 62b)

(c) **Space** — The encounter of positive and negative unit forms (resulting in subtraction) is a way of producing spatial contrast. Space can be pushed and squeezed by unit forms which are thrust against each other. It can also be left void, in contrast with congested areas. (Fig. 62c)

(d) **Gravity** — Unit forms dropping from high to low positions, or stacking from low to high positions, can suggest a gravitational pull. Stable and unstable unit forms, static and moving unit forms, or heavy and light unit forms can be put together in effective contrast of gravity. (Fig. 62d)

Dominance and Emphasis

Two factors should be considered in a contrast structure:

Dominance of majority — Dominance is gained by one kind of unit form which occupies more space in a design than other kinds. These unit forms, as distinguished from all others by shape, size, color, texture, direction, position, space, and/or gravity, are in a majority because they are spread over a wider area. Dominance of majority helps to pull the design together into an integrated whole.

Emphasis of minority — Dominance of majority does not necessarily put the minority into oblivion. On the contrary, the minority often gets emphasized and demands greater attention. It is like an anomaly, which is more readily seen.

Dominance of majority and emphasis of minority normally work together in a contrast structure. Even if there is only one kind of unit form in the design, various relational elements can be manipulated to create dominance and emphasis. Dominance of majority is like the heavier weight, closer to the fulcrum, and emphasis of minority like the lighter weight, farther away from the fulcrum, establishing a balance as illustrated in figure **61b**.

Notes on the Exercises

Figures **63a, b, c, d, e, f, g,** and **h** are all examples of contrast structures. There are two kinds of unit form used: one kind is rectilinear, the other kind curvilinear. The two kinds are in contrast of shape and sometimes of size as well. They meet each other, creating new shapes by union or subtraction. Both kinds are allowed to change in shape within a certain range of similarity, and in size even more flexibly.

Note the use of contrast in each of the examples.

a

b

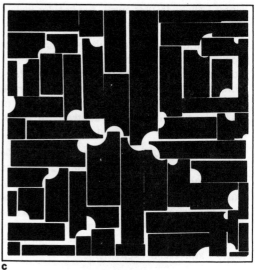

c

d

e

g

f

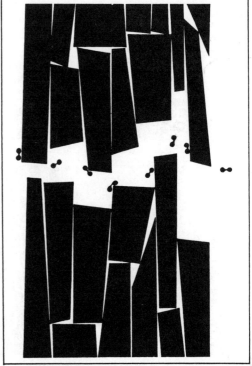

h

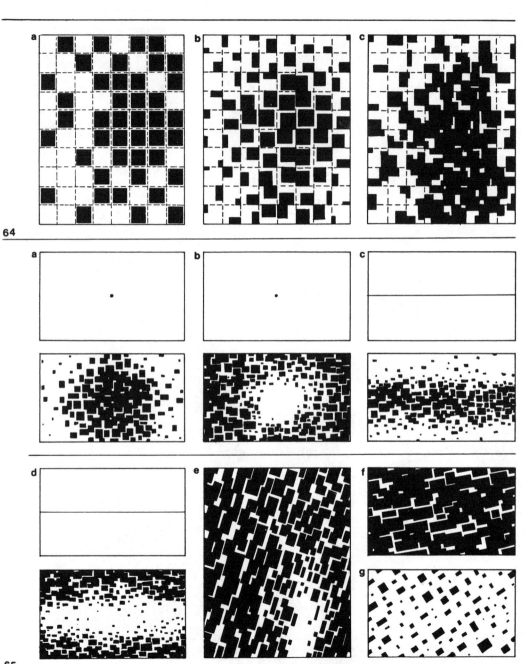

64

65

CHAPTER 10: CONCENTRATION

Concentration refers to a way of distribution of unit forms which may be thickly gathered in certain areas or thinly scattered in other areas of a design. The distribution is usually uneven and informal, sometimes with one place of thickest gathering or thinnest scattering which becomes the center of interest.

In our environment, the city is a typical example of concentration. Buildings and people crowd around the heart of every city, while they are gradually thinned down towards the outskirts.

Essentially concentration is quantitative organization. Here the designer is concerned with the quantity of unit forms producing rhythmic accentuations or dramatic tensions by varying from one place to the next. Contrast is involved, but it is a contrast of less and more rather than a contrast of visual or relational elements.

Concentration of Unit Forms in Formal Structures

The effect of concentration can be created even within formal structures without changing the rigid structural discipline. Movement of unit forms is much restricted by the structural subdivisions which also govern the area occupied by each unit form and the directions of arrangement, but concentration can be made via one of the following ways:

Frequent absences — As we have seen as early as Chapter 2, when the unit form is of the same color as the ground, it can disappear without affecting the general discipline. Thus frequent absences can result in uneven distribution of unit forms, leading to concentration in certain places in a design. The pattern of absences can be irregular or quite regular, depending on how much regularity the designer chooses to maintain in the design. (Fig. **64a**)

Positional changes — Positional changes of unit forms inside active structural subdivisions can increase or decrease the proportion of occupied space as against unoccupied space. The effect of concentration occurs when there is more occupied space in one area surrounded by more unoccupied space in other areas. Directional changes can sometimes produce the same results. Regular gradational changes should be avoided in such cases. (Fig. **64b**)

Quantitative changes — If the size of unit forms is rather small, one structural subdivision can house several of them conveniently. In this way actual quantitative changes can be made with some structural subdivisions containing one or none, others containing two or more unit forms. The effect of concentration can be achieved, but the structural subdivisions should be active, otherwise the structure would show no effect at all in the final design. Again, regular gradational changes should be avoided if we are after a concentration design and not a gradation design. (Fig. **64c**)

We should note that among the different types of formal structure, the repetition structure provides the greatest flexibility for the effect of concentration. Both gradation and radiation structures, owing to their intrinsic qualities, have a predetermined area (or areas) of concentration, departure from which would be difficult if not impossible.

When there is more than just one kind of unit form in a design, concentration of one kind and dispersion of another (or others) can produce effects of dominance and emphasis.

In concentration, each visual or relational element can be considered separately. For instance, in a repetition structure the unit forms can be repetitive in all elements except color, which may be distributed concentratively.

The Concentration Structure

When a formal structure is not used, unit forms can be freely organized to achieve the effect of concentration. This produces a concentration structure which is entirely informal. Sometimes a formal structure may be used just to provide some guidelines for the distribution of unit forms. Concentration structures of this kind can be said to be semi-formal.

The kinds of concentration structures are suggested as follows:

(a) **Concentration towards a point** — This means that the unit forms crowd around a pre-established conceptual point in a design. The density reaches the maximum where the point lies and gradually thins down in surrounding areas. The effect is a sort of informal radiation, and more so if the directions of the unit forms are arranged radiatively. The number of pre-established points can range from one to many which may be guided by a formal structure. The degree of concentration towards each point can be uniformly similar, alternatively similar, vaguely gradational, or all different. (Fig. **65a**)

(b) **Concentration away from a point** — This is the reverse of (a), with blankness or extreme scantiness in the immediate areas surrounding the conceptual point. (Fig. **65b**)

(c) **Concentration towards a line** — This means that the unit forms crowd around a pre-established conceptual line in a design. Maximum density occurs along the line. The line can be straight or of any simple shape. When more than one pre-established line is used, they may be structural lines of a formal structure. Concentration towards a line approaches the effect of gradation. (Fig. **65c**)

(d) **Concentration away from a line** — This is the reverse of (c), with blankness or extreme scantiness in the immediate area of the line. (Fig. **65d**)

(e) **Free concentration** — This means that the unit forms are grouped freely with varying density and scantiness in the design. Organization is completely informal here, very much as in a contrast structure. Contrast of less and more p. evails, but it should be carefully handled to create visual subtlety and/or drama. (Fig. **65e**)

(f) **Over-concentration** — This means that the unit forms are grouped densely over the entire design, or over a rather wide area of the design, with or without gradual transition at the edges. If the unit forms are of similar size and grouped quite evenly, the result of over-concentration can become a similarity structure wherein each unit form occupies a similar amount of space. (Fig. **65f**)

(g) **Deconcentration** — This is the reverse of (f). Here the unit forms never get concentrated in any place, but are thinly scattered over the entire design, or over a rather wide area. The scattering can be even, uneven, subtly rhythmical, or vaguely gradational. A similar structure can result if the unit forms, of similar size, are scattered quite evenly. (Fig. **65g**)

Unit Forms in Concentration Structures

The effect of concentration is better achieved if all the unit forms are of relatively small size so that a large quantity of them can be used to build up the density desired at suitable places. Size thus becomes the first element to be considered and shape only secondary. If the size of unit forms is generally large and its variation covers a wide range, the result may be a contrast structure rather than a concentration structure.

The shapes of the unit forms do not have to be all of one kind. Two or more kinds can be used, and the unit forms of each kind, among themselves, may be used in repetition or in similarity. If the shapes show a sense of direction, they can be arranged so that their directions may be repetitive, gradational, radiative, or just random.

Notes on the Exercises

Figures **66a, b, c, d, e, f, g**, and **h** all exemplify the use of concentration structure. The unit forms are mostly organic, with variations in shape and size within a moderate range of similarity. It should not be difficult for us to recognize which kind of concentration structure is used in each exercise.

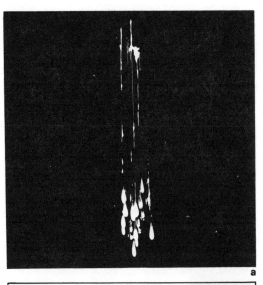

a

b

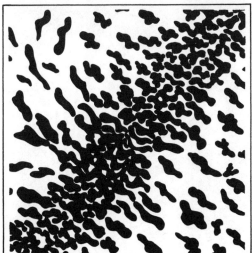

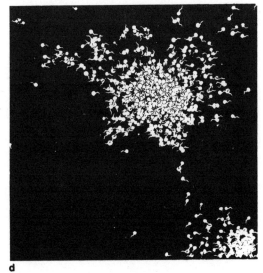

c

d

66

e

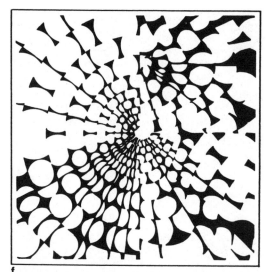

f

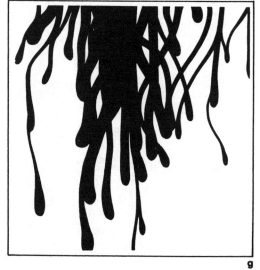

g

h

CHAPTER 11: TEXTURE

Texture is one visual element which has been mentioned frequently but never fully discussed in the preceding chapters. This is because the exercises are limited to uniform black and white surfaces, and the use of texture has been completely excluded. Texture, however, has unique aspects which are essential in certain design situations and should not be overlooked.

Early in Chapter 1, it was pointed out that texture refers to the surface characteristics of a shape. Every shape has a surface and every surface must have certain characteristics, which may be described as smooth or rough, plain or decorated, matt or glossy, soft or hard. Although we generally regard a flat painted surface as containing no texture at all, actually the flatness of the paint is a kind of texture, and there is also the texture of the material on which the shape is created.

Nature contains a wealth of textures. For instance, each kind of stone or wood possesses a distinct texture which an architect or an interior designer may choose for specific purposes. The piece of stone or wood may also be finished in a multiple of ways for diverse textural effects.

Texture may be classified into two important categories: visual texture and tactile texture. Appropriate texture adds richness to a design.

Visual Texture

Visual texture is strictly two-dimensional. As the term implies, it is the kind of texture that is seen by the eye, although it also may evoke tactile sensations. Three kinds of visual textures can be distinguished:

Decorative texture — This decorates a surface, and remains subordinate to shape. In other words, the texture itself is only an addition which can be removed without much affecting the shapes and their interrelationships in the design. It can be hand-drawn or obtained by special devices and can be rigidly regular or irregular, but it generally maintains a certain degree of uniformity. (Fig. **67a**)

Spontaneous texture — This does not decorate a surface, but is part of the process of visual creation. Shape and texture cannot be separated, because the marks of texture on a surface are the shapes at the same time. Hand-drawn and accidental forms frequently contain spontaneous texture. (Fig. **67b**)

Mechanical texture — This does not refer to texture obtained with the aid of mechanical drawing instruments such as the ruler or compasses. It refers to texture obtained by special mechanical means, and as a result, the texture is not necessarily subordinate to shape. A typical example of this kind of texture is the photographic grain or screen pattern we often find in printing. Mechanical texture can also be found in designs created by typography, and in computer graphics. (Fig. **67c**)

The Making of Visual Texture

Visual texture can be produced in various ways. Some common techniques are suggested as follows:

(a) **Drawing, painting** — These are the simplest methods of producing visual texture. Minute drawn or painted patterns can be constructed of densely gathered, tiny unit forms in rigid or loose structures for the surface decoration of any form. Spontaneous texture can be obtained with freely hand-drawn lines or brushstrokes. (Fig. **68a**)

(b) **Printing, transferring, rubbing** — a carved pattern or a rough surface can be inked and printed on another surface to create a visual texture which may be decorative or spontaneous depending on how the technique is handled. Hand-painted images on one surface can be transferred to another surface when the paint is still wet. Rubbing with pencil or any suitable medium on soft and thin paper over a rough surface also produces textural effects. (Fig. **68b**)

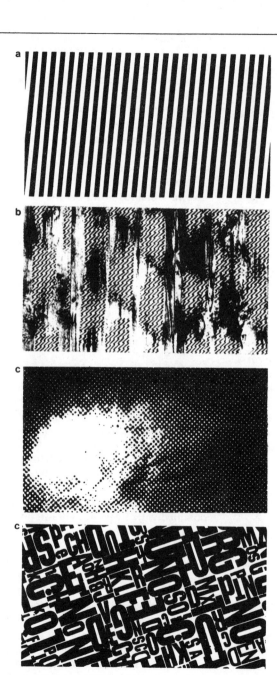

(c) **Spraying, spilling, pouring** — Liquid paint, diluted or evaporated to any desired consistency, may be sprayed, spilled, or poured onto a surface. Spontaneous texture is often obtained, but carefully controlled spraying can produce decorative texture as well. (Fig. **68c**)

(d) **Staining, dyeing** — An absorbent surface may be stained or dyed to obtain a kind of visual texture. (Fig. **68d**)

(e) **Smoking, burning** — A surface can be smoked over a flame to obtain a kind of texture. Sometimes burnt marks may also be utilized. (Fig. **68e**)

(f) **Scratching, scraping** — A painted or inked surface can be scratched or scraped with some kind of hard or sharp tool to gain in texture. (Fig. **68f**)

(g) **Photographic processes** — Special darkroom techniques can add interesting texture to photographic images. (Fig. **68g**)

Collage

A direct way of using visual texture in a design is collage, which is a process of pasting, glueing, or fixing pieces of paper, fabric, or other flat materials onto a surface. Such materials may fall into three main groups according to whether images are present or important. The term "image" here refers to any printed, photographic, painted, or intentional or accidental forms or marks on the surface of the materials.

Materials without images — These materials are evenly colored or of uniform texture. The shapes of the cut or torn pieces are the only shapes to appear in the design. Examples of such materials are paper or fabric with solid color or minute patterns which spread rather regularly all over the surface, printed sheets of crowded, small type, selected areas from photographs or surfaces containing spontaneous texture with all contrasts minimized. (Fig. **69a**)

Materials with images — These materials, such as paper or fabric printed with uneven patterns or treated with spontaneous texture, photographs with strong tonal or color contrasts, printed sheets of large type or large and small type, etc., contain images of considerable prominence. Such images are used abstractly in the collage, regardless of any representational or literal content. They are seen as forms which are as important as, and sometimes even more important than, the shapes of the cut or torn materials. (Fig. **69b**)

Materials with essential images — Images on the materials are essential when they have a definite representational content or when the images have to maintain their identity and are not to be destroyed during the process of the collage. In this case they are more important than the cut or torn shapes of the materials, and the collage is thus of a different nature. Materials with representational significance are commonly photographs which can be dissected and rearranged or combined with other photographs for dramatic purposes or special effects. Materials with abstract images can be dissected and rearranged in the same way, resulting in transformations or distortions without rendering the original images unrecognizable. (Fig. **69c**)

Tactile Texture

Tactile texture is a kind of texture that is not only visible to the eye but can be felt with the hand. Tactile texture rises above the surface of a two-dimensional design and approaches a three-dimensional relief.

Broadly speaking, tactile texture exists in all types of surfaces because we can feel them. This means all kinds of paper, however smooth, and all kinds of paint and ink, however flat, have their specific surface characteristics which can be discerned by the sense of touch. In two-dimensional design, we can say that a blank area or a solidly printed or painted area contains no visual texture, but there is always the tactile texture of the paper and the ink or paint.

To narrow down its scope, we can limit our discussion to the kinds of tactile texture specially created by the designer for the purpose. This means the materials have been specially

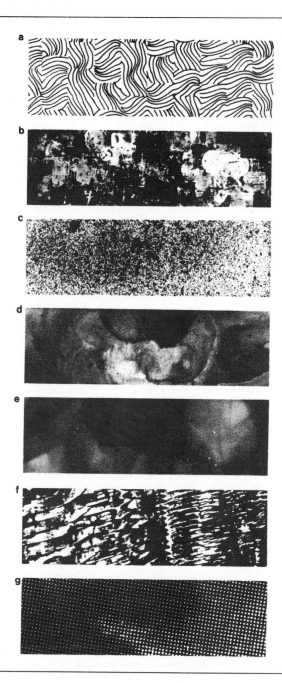

shaped or arranged, or combined with other materials, to form a composition, or the materials have undergone special treatment, resulting in new textural sensations. Thus we can have three distinct kinds of tactile texture:

Available natural texture — The natural texture of the materials is maintained. The materials, which may be paper, fabric, branches, leaves, sand, strings, etc., are cut, torn, or used as they are, and pasted, glued, or fixed onto a surface. No effort is made to hide the identity on the materials.

Modified natural texture — The materials are modified so that they are not the same as usual. For instance, paper is not pasted flat but creased or crumpled, or it can be stippled, scratched, embossed. A piece of sheet metal can be folded, hammered, or drilled with tiny holes. A piece of wood can be carved. The materials are slightly transformed, but not beyond recognition. (Fig. **70a**)

Organized texture — The materials, usually in small bits, chips, or strips, are organized into a pattern which forms a new surface. The textural units may be used as they are or modified, but they must be small or cut into small pieces. Examples of these are seeds, grains of sand, chips of wood, leaves cut into very narrow strips, paper twisted into tiny balls, pins, beads, buttons, strings or threads to be woven, etc. The materials may sometimes be identifiable, but the new surface sensation is much more dominant. (Fig. **70b**)

All kinds of tactile texture can be transformed into visual texture by the photographic process.

Light and Color in Tactile Texture

The play of light upon a tactile texture may be very interesting. Certain materials may reflect or refract light, with fascinating results. The tactile quality of rough surfaces is usually emphasized by strong side-lighting.

Some designs may have been conceived with light modulation as an essential element. In this case, the textural units are usually long and thin, projecting from the surface of the support material, so that shadows are rather linear, forming intricate patterns.

However, it should be pointed out that both light and shadow are visual, not tactile, because they have nothing to do with the sense of touch. Programmed lighting and changing relationships of the light source and the design can produce kinetic light patterns, but still the effect is a pure visual sensation.

Color can also play an interesting role in tactile texture. The natural color of the materials can be maintained, but a coat of color can create a different feeling, at least rendering the materials less immediately recognizable, giving them less of an available natural texture but more of a modified natural texture. Diverse materials on a surface can resemble each other if they are all coated with the same color.

When there is more than one color on a surface, the colors will form a pattern which is visual. Sometimes the visual pattern can dominate over the sensation provoked by the tactile texture.

Notes on the Exercises

Figures **71a, b, c, d, e, f, g,** and **h** all show the use of printed type to form textural patterns. Single characters of large type or lines of small type from printed matter have been specially cut and arranged so that blank spaces are eliminated as far as possible. Type of the same size and weight can be grouped to form a uniform texture, while a gradational texture can be created with type of varying size and weight.

Some of the examples were done by gathering and arranging type to form a uniform or gradational texture on a thin sheet of paper. This was later cut into pieces for final organization into a structured pattern.

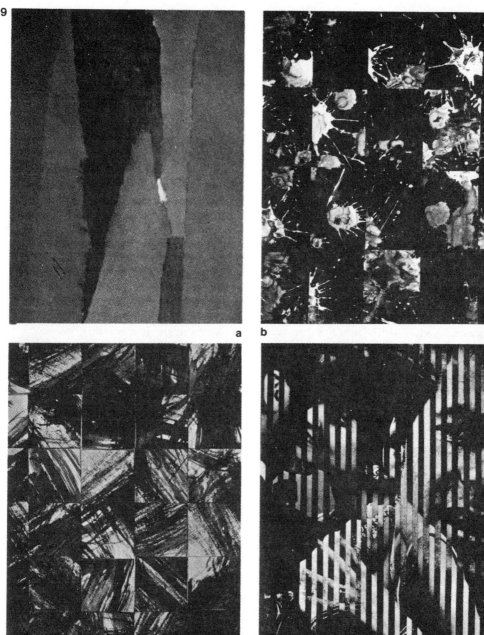

69

a

b

b

c

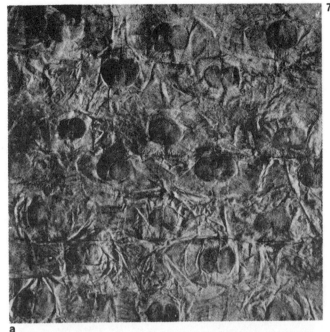

a

b

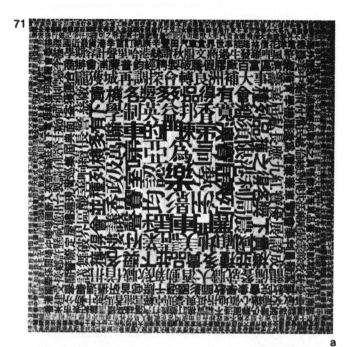

a

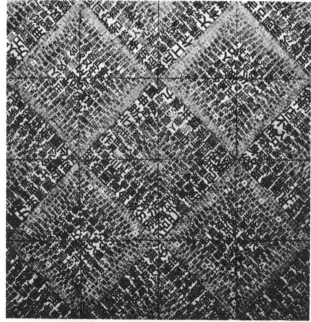

b

c

e

d

f

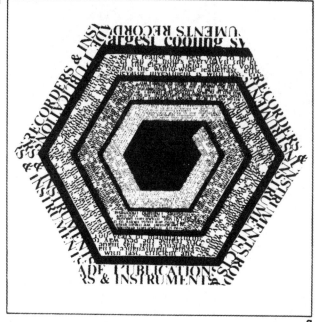

g

h

CHAPTER 12: SPACE

Space, like texture in the preceding chapter, has been mentioned in almost every chapter but has never been fully discussed. The nature of space is rather complex because there are many ways space can be viewed. Space may be positive or negative, flat or illusory, ambiguous, or conflicting. Each of these aspects will be carefully examined here.

Positive and Negative Space

Positive space is what surrounds a negative form, and negative space is what surrounds a positive form. Positive and negative forms were discussed in Chapter 2 (fig. **8**). All positive forms contain positive space, but positive space is not always perceived as a positive form. Similarly, all negative forms contain negative space, but negative space is not always perceived as a negative form. This is because positive space can be a background for negative forms and negative space for positive forms, and backgrounds are not normally recognized as forms which usually exist in a certain degree of isolation.

Of course, positive (or negative) space completely or nearly isolated by negative (or positive) forms can be identified as positive (or negative) form, but such forms are generally very much hidden unless we consciously look for them. If they are found frequently and regularly, then the figure-ground relationship is reversible: at one moment we find positive forms and negative space, at another moment we find negative forms and positive space. (Fig. **72a**)

Flat and Illusory Space

Space is flat when all the forms seem to lie on the picture plane and be parallel to it. The forms themselves should be flat too, and appear equidistant from the eye, none nearer and none farther. It is possible, however, that we can feel the space surrounding the forms to be very deep, leaving all the forms floating on the picture plane.

In a flat space situation, forms can meet one another by touching, penetration, union, subtraction, intersection, coinciding, or just be in detachment, but they can never meet by overlapping. (Fig. **72b**) Overlapping suggests that one form is nearer to our eyes than another, thus rendering the space illusory to some extent. (Fig. **72c**) Variations in shape, size, color, and texture may also destroy the flatness of space, but this does not always happen.

Space is illusory when all the forms seem not to lie on or be parallel to the picture plane. Some forms may appear to advance, some to recede, some to present their frontal views, and some to show their oblique views. The forms themselves may be flat or three-dimensional. The design area opens up like a window or a stage where the forms are displayed in varying depths and/or at different angles. (Fig. **72d**)

Flat Forms in Illusory Space

Forms are considered flat when they have no apparent thickness. Flat forms in illusory space are like forms made of thin sheets of paper, metal, or other materials. Their frontal views are the fullest, occupying the largest area. Their oblique views are narrowed, and occupy less area. The following are some common ways flat forms can be used in illusory space:

(a) **Overlapping** — When one form overlaps another, it is seen as being in front of or above the other. The flat forms may have no appreciable thickness at all, but if overlapping occurs, one of the two forms must have some diversion from the picture plane, however slight the diversion may be. (Fig. **73a**)

(b) **Change in size** — Increase in size of a form suggests that it is getting nearer, whereas decrease in its size suggests that it is farther away. The greater the range of change in size

a

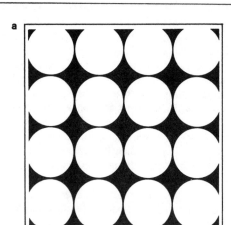

b

c

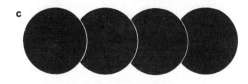

d

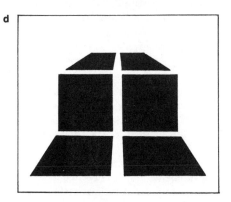

present in the design, the deeper is the illusion of spatial depth. (Fig. **73b**)

(c) **Change in color** — On a white background, darker colors stand out much more than lighter colors, thus appearing closer to our eyes. On a very dark background, the reverse is true. If both warm and cool colors are present in a design, generally the warm colors appear to advance whereas the cool ones recede. (Fig. **73c**)

(d) **Change in texture** — Coarser textures normally appear closer to our eyes than finer textures. (Fig. **73d**)

(e) **Change in view** — A form is in full frontal view when it is parallel to the picture plane. If it is not parallel to the picture plane, we can only see it from a slanting angle. Change in view is a result of spatial rotation (see Chapter 6, section on spatial gradation), creating illusory space though not a very deep one. (Fig. **73e**)

(f) **Curving or bending** — Flat forms can be curved or bent to suggest illusory space. Curving or bending changes their absolute frontality and activates their diversion from the picture plane. (Fig. **73f**)

(g) **Addition of shadow** — The addition of a shadow to a form emphasizes the physical existence of the form. The shadow may be cast in front of or behind the form, linked to or detached from it. (Fig. **73g**)

Volume and Depth in Illusory Space

All flat forms can become three-dimensional forms in illusory space with the suggestion of thickness, which just requires supplementary views added to the frontal view. As a three-dimensional form is not always seen in full frontality, there are many angles and points of view from which it can be seen and represented on a flat surface convincingly. (Fig. **74a**)

There are isometric and other systems of projection in the representation of volume and depth. (Fig. **74b**) There are also laws of perspective by means of which we can depict volume and depth with a surprising degree of realism. (Fig. **74c**) If we have to represent a cube that has six equal edges meeting each other at right angles, simple systems of projection maintain the equality of the edges and angles to some extent, but perspective which gives a more convincing picture renders most of the equal elements unequal.

When a series of cubes is to be represented with one behind another, no decrease in size of the cubes is shown with the various systems of projection, but a gradational decrease in size is shown with perspective. (Fig. **74d**)

Plane Representation in Illusory Space

Volume is contained by planes which can be represented in various ways:

(a) **Outlined planes** — Planes can be outlined, and the designer may choose any thickness of line for his purpose. Outlined planes in illusory space are usually represented as opaque planes: we cannot see what is behind them. If they are represented as transparent planes, then they may become more like spatial frames. (Fig. **75a**)

(b) **Solid planes** — These are planes without ambiguity. Solid planes, if they are of the same color, can be used as flat forms to suggest illusory depth, but it is difficult for them to work together to suggest volume. Solid planes with color variations can represent volume with great effectiveness. (Fig. **75b**)

(c) **Uniformly textured planes** — A uniformly textured plane is distinguishable from another which it adjoins or overlaps even if the texture of the two planes is the same. This is because the textural pattern of one plane does not have to spread continuously to the plane adjacent to it. Certain kinds of texture have strong directional feeling which can give emphasis to planes that is not seen frontally but sideways. Densely spaced parallel lines of the same width or regular dot patterns can form textural planes which provide many possibilities for the designer. (Fig. **75c**)

(d) **Gradationally colored or textured**

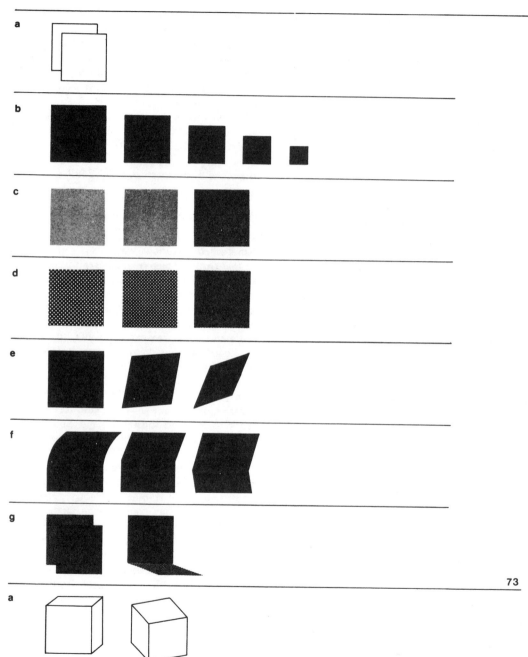

planes — Gradationally colored or textured planes have a different effect in the creation of spatial illusion. They suggest light and shadow patterns or metallic sheens on surfaces, thus enhancing realism to some extent. They are particularly effective in the representation of curved surfaces. (Fig. **75d**) Textured planes in perspective should be depicted in such a way that the textural patterns are also seen in perspective. Such textured planes are not uniform but gradational and even radiative (radiating from the vanishing points).

Fluctuating and Conflicting Space

Space fluctuates when it appears to advance at one moment and recede at another moment. We have already mentioned a kind of simple fluctuating situation when we discussed positive and negative space and reversible figure-ground relationships earlier in this chapter (fig. **72a**). A more dynamic fluctuating situation is illustrated in figure **76a**, which can be interpreted either as a shape that is seen from above or as a shape seen from below. Both interpretations are valid. Spatial fluctuation creates interesting optical movements.

Conflicting space is similar to fluctuating space yet intrinsically different. Fluctuating space is ambiguous, because there is not a definite way whereby we can interpret the spatial situation, but conflicting space provides an absurd spatial situation which seems impossible for us to interpret at all. In conflicting space, we feel we are definitely looking down if we only see one part of the design, and we feel we are definitely looking up if we only see another part of the design. However, when the design is seen as a whole, the two visual experiences are in serious conflict with each other and cannot be reconciled. The situation is absurd because it does not exist in reality. Somehow it evokes a strange visual tension which offers many interesting possibilities for artists and designers. (Fig. **76b**)

Notes on the Exercises

Various types of illusory space are depicted in figures **77a, b, c, d, e, f, g,** and **h.** The planes are constructed of regular line patterns, some repetitive, some gradational.

If we review all the exercises illustrated in this book, we can, in fact, discover more examples depicting illusory space. Figure **26f** suggests a solid sphere. Figures **47g** and **h** both show curved surfaces; figures **55b** and **j** appear to be reliefs, and there are still more.

The exercises, from Chapter 3 to the present chapter, represent a journey the reader has made. He will see that the earlier exercises generally have greater restrictions, demanding more specific unit forms, whereas the later exercises provide greater freedom. On the whole, the exercises demand both a disciplined mind and hand, which are necessary equipment for a designer. Creative artists may not find doing all the exercises enjoyable, but the exercises do suggest possibilities as well as limitations. Visual grammar is only a basic tool; the full realm of creativity is to be explored by each individual.

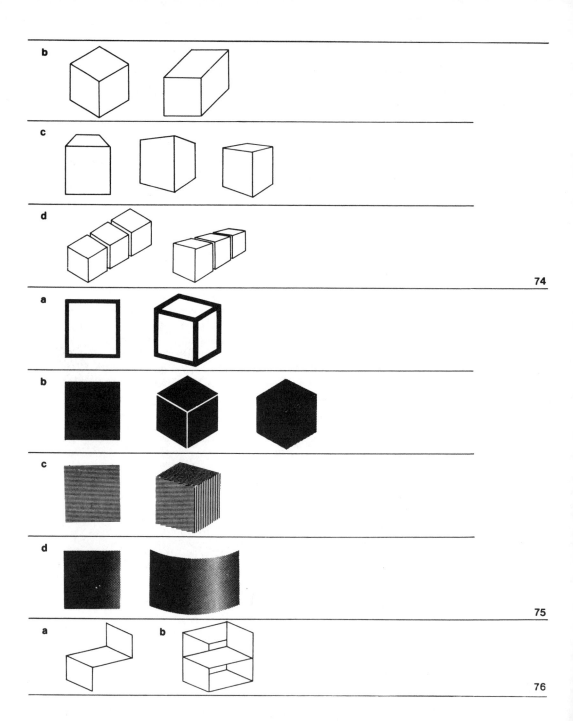

b

c

d

74

a

b

c

d

75

a   **b**

76

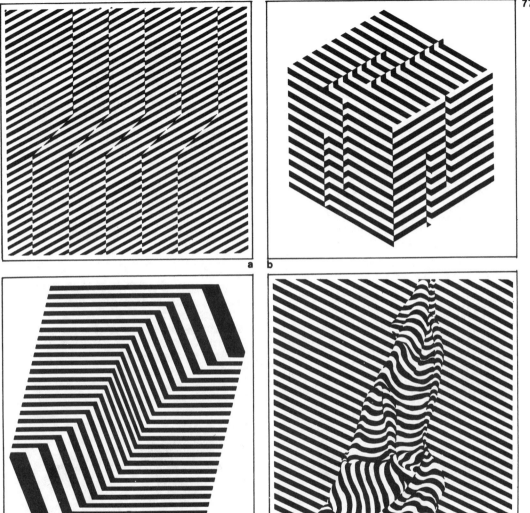

a　b

c　d

e f

g h